The Afrofuturism Cyclicality of Past, Present, and Future in Kendrick Lamar's *To Pimp a Butterfly*

Jack J Nielsen

Contents:

1	Introduction		3-10
	Afrofuturism in Hip Hop		5
2	Kendrick Lamar: The Pimp or the Butterfly?		11-26
	Conscious Rap Background		14
	Critical Reception of Conscious Rap		17
	To Pimp a Butterfly: How *To Pimp a Butterfly* Tackles the Music (Rap) Industry		21
3	Multi-Ego: Multi-Consciousness and the Many Personas of Kendrick Lamar		27-50
	The Negative Internalization of Depression		30
	Time Travel Identity Exploration		37
	The External Pressures of Speaking For the People		42
	Kendrick vs. Lucy/Lucifer/America/Music Industry		48
4	Moving at a Meteor Speed: Time Travelling through the History of Afrofuturist Music 51-69		
	Future from the Past: George Clinton		52
	Past Meets Present: The Jazz of Thundercat, Kamasi Washington, Robert Glasper, Terrance Martin, and Ambrose Akinmusire		65
	Present Meets Future: The New Generation and the Electronic Music of Flying Lotus, Thundercat, and Pharrell Williams		71
5	The Politics of Always, Now, and Forever: How To Pimp a Butterfly Tackles the Past, Present, and Future of Racial Politics		74-118
	Addressing the Caterpillar in the Room: Reimagining the Realistic Past of African-American History		78
	Kendrick's Past		84

        Ain't Nothin' Changed: Connecting the Past with the Present
        89

        The Present State of Race in America: Black Lives Matter
        90

        The Future is Now, The Future is Next   107

        Pulling from the Past to Imagine the Future: An Afrofuturist's Guide   111

6   God Is Gangsta: The Religion of To Pimp a Butterfly   119-130

        To Battle the Devil, You Better Have Some Power   120

        Kendrick's Complicated Relationship with Lucy   123

        Kendrick as Preacher and Prophet on his own Journey for Peace with Religion   128

7   Returning Home to Family   131-140

        King Kendrick of Compton   132

        Tupac: A Conversation with His Successor   134

        Returning Home to Momma and Mother Africa   138

8   Epilogue   141-143

    Bibliography   144-147

1.

Introduction

The caterpillar is a prisoner to the streets that conceived it. Its only job is to eat or consume everything around it, in order to protect itself from this mad city. While consuming its environment the caterpillar begins to notice ways to survive. One thing it noticed is how much the world shuns him, but praises the butterfly. The butterfly represents the talent, the thoughtfulness, and the beauty within the caterpillar. But having a harsh outlook on life the caterpillar sees the butterfly as weak and figures out a way to pimp it to his own benefits. Already surrounded by this mad city, the caterpillar goes to work on the cocoon which institutionalizes him. He can no longer see past his own thoughts. He's trapped. When trapped inside these walls certain ideas take root, such as going home, and bringing back new concepts to this mad city. The result? Wings begin to emerge, breaking the cycle of feeling stagnant. Finally free, the butterfly sheds light on situations that the caterpillar never considered, ending the internal struggle. Although the butterfly and caterpillar are completely different, they are one and the same.

-"Mortal Man" Kendrick Lamar

In December of 2015, President Barack Obama told People Magazine that his favorite song of the year was Kendrick Lamar's "How Much a Dollar Cost".[1] The track, a self-revelatory story in which Kendrick Lamar comes across a homeless man at a gas station who begs for money, alludes to the parable in Matthew 25:40 in which Jesus decides who he will take to Heaven. Kendrick's faith and Christian

---

[1] Tierney McAfee, "Kendrick Lamar Vs. Bruno Mars: POTUS and FLOTUS' Favorite Songs, Movies and Moments of 2015," *People.com*, December 9, 2015.

fortitude are tested, as he refuses to give the homeless man money because he thinks the man is a drug addict. However, the end of the track reveals the homeless man to be God in disguise and the plea for charity a test that Kendrick fails, ultimately costing him a place in Heaven.

Just as Barack Obama's election as President of the United States and leader of the free world was a monumental and unprecedented moment in the history of the country and black America specifically, to a lesser extent, Obama admitting that he listens to, enjoys, and is likely influenced morally by a rapper from Compton is another unprecedented and monumental moment for African-American art. Although hip hop is academically taught in universities and generally respected as an accurate portrayal of the life and times of a faction of oppressed and marginalized black youth, politicians (and most certainly Presidents) have historically dismissed the art form as vulgar, destructive of traditional American values, and even worthy of being banned from cultural consumption. For Obama to recognize the artistry and importance of Kendrick Lamar's personal, political, and religious messages in *To Pimp a Butterfly*, parallels and highlights a cultural shift towards acceptance of one of the most important and popular expressions of African-American art. Not only did the album encourage President Obama to invite Lamar to meet with him in the Oval Office, but Kendrick also performed with the National Symphony Orchestra in Washington D.C. These accomplishments are seemingly just the beginning of the catapulting of Kendrick's conscious and politically charged hip hop into the forefront of American culture and politicized issues of race.

"How Much a Dollar Cost" is a moral tale of charity, humility, and trust in the word of God to help those that are less fortunate and, although this is one of many internal struggles Kendrick wrestles with throughout his groundbreaking album, it is not a stretch to imagine that President Obama was inspired and influenced by a multitude of the messages found in the album. As this book will show, Kendrick Lamar's *To Pimp a Butterfly* is one of the most important and apt works of African-American art of its time. A time-travelling, metamophorisizing, genre-encompassing, Afrofuturist message of the African-American experience that reimagines and pulls from the past, situates itself firmly in the present, and imagines a brighter future for African-American people and culture.

Afrofuturism in Hip Hop

How do you know I'm real? I'm not real. I'm just like you. You don't exist in this society. If you did, your people wouldn't be seeking equal rights. You're not real. If you were, you'd have some status among the nations of the world. I come to you as the myth, because that's what black people are. I came from a dream that a black man dreamed long ago.[2]

-Sun Ra, Space Is The Place (1972)

Afrofuturism is dark matter moving at the speed of light. It's dealing with a cosmic force of showing indigenous people, from the motherland, cause Zulu said they come from Mars, [...] taking people on a soul sonic trip to the universe, where everything is open and free.[3]

-Afrika Bambaataa

In an article and interview that serves as one of the central starting points for Afrofuturism, author and culture critic Mark Dery offers the analogy that African-Americans are the descendants of the

---

[2] *Space Is The Place,* directed by John Coney (1974; USA: Harte Recordings, 2015), DVD.
[3] "Afrika Bambaataa on Afrofuturism," BFI.org, accessed December 4, 2014.

first alien abductees, taken from their home planet (Africa), placed on spaceships (large boats unfamiliar to the Africans sold into slavery), and taken to another planet (America) to be branded, bred, enslaved, and experimented on. Dery and his interviewees, including science fiction author Samuel Delany, discuss how and why African-Americans had been previously written out of, ignored, or dismissed within the genre of science/speculative fiction.

Even though in the landmark interview Dery and company are discussing the exclusion of black authors from and representation within sf (science/speculative fiction) works and culture, Afrofuturist musicians have utilized this exclusion to their advantage as a way to escape an American society and culture that has historically ostracized them as a people. Since the slave trade and subsequent adaptation into American life was, as Dery writes, "a sci fi nightmare in which unseen but no less impassable force fields of intolerance frustrate their movement; official histories undo what has been done; and technology is too often brought to bear on black bodies"[4] African-Americans have often found difficulty in trying to hold on to the traditions of their ancestors while living in a land that seems to systematically erase that history. Whether it is an attempt of early 20th century western critics to discredit "primitive" aspects of African tradition or throw historical shade over the ugly scars of the slave days, African-American history is something that the black community has historically had to hold onto lest it be lost by coming generations. As we now know, African culture was not erased during slavery as individuals and groups were able to preserve certain traditions through what African-American studies giant Melville Herskovits calls "African cultural retentions", even if some of those cultural forms were often changed or lost. Ultimately, and to the credit of the strength of oppressed slaves, many of these cultural retentions permeate African-American life since slavery and among the African Diaspora.

---

[4] Dery, Mark. "Black to the Future: Interviews with Samuel R. Delany, Greg Tate, and Tricia Rose." edited by Dery, Mark, 179-222: Duke UP, 1994. Web. 28 January 2014.

The issue that brought the concept and popularity of Afrofuturism to fruition is that, like most modes of artistic expression throughout the history of the United States, black contributions are often ignored or purposefully effaced by the status quo in a given cultural movement. This has been apparent since slave traders attempted to eliminate connections that blacks had to African traditions, family, or spiritual beliefs up to the rise in popularity of jazz and rock n' roll which is rooted in African-American expression but has been historically beneficial financially to white artists with greater social, political, and business influence. Not to say that all white sf writers purposefully or maliciously omitted black characters from their work, but it is important to point out that not only has it been an arduous struggle for the sf community to critically accept work that imagines a future where black characters survive and thrive, it has been an ongoing battle for black sf authors to become more accepted into the artistic community of sf, which has been historically adept at addressing issues perceived as progressive politics. Unfortunately, popular sf works rarely included overtly black characters, instead choosing to replace them with alien beings and subsequently failing to appropriately and successfully depict relatable associations with alienation. Given the analogy that African-Americans are descendants of the first alien abductees, it is only logical that African-American artists would find creative avenues within sf to not only reclaim the past that has been purposefully discounted, but to depict black figures and a black community as a prevalent part of the imagined future. This bi-directionality gives Afrofuturist artists license to explore and utilize not only the entire history of African and African-American culture, but to muse upon and express an imagined future for black people. Afrofuturism is a direct response to a lack of black presence in conceptions of the future and/or representations of it in which black bodies are replaced by alien bodies, but it can also work as a re-envisioning of a past in which black bodies were subjected, discounted, discriminated against and ostracized.

Ytasha Womack contends that author Octavia Butler and musicians Sun Ra and George Clinton make up the holy trinity of

Afrofuturist art.[5] Although Afrofuturism as an aesthetic movement and list-serve conversation began as a discussion about African-American representation in sf, it is an equally effective way to approach African-American music and since popular music reaches a broader audience than a work of sf, Womack's assessment of two musicians as pillars of the movement is appropriate. Afrofuturism can take on many forms of artistic expression besides literature and music such as visual art and film; however, it is music in which black artists have made the greatest social and cultural impact within American popular culture. Whereas in literature, visual art, and film, black artists continue to progress yet struggle to gain equal recognition within the historically white dominated critical gaze of American culture, black music has had an undeniable meteoric rise in popularity, often dominating critical evaluation and the financial success of the worldwide popular charts. Sun Ra and George Clinton took on alien identities, blurring the lines between fiction and reality to propel the Afrofuturist aesthetic into the mainstream culture. As revolutionary figures in the production and live performance of music, they flipped the script on the idea that Otherness was a negative association while making weird and/or alien identities cool to their fans rather than something negative to the individual or communal self-esteem.

Not only do Afrofuturist musicians maintain the traditions of their African and African-American ancestors by incorporating elements of blues, jazz, soul, and rock n' roll into their craft, but by utilizing the Afrofuturist aesthetic to place these elements within a futurist framework, they are removing their art from the destructive past of American history. George Clinton once said that he "had to find another place where they [white people/American artists] hadn't perceived black people to be and that was on a spaceship"[6] indicating a removal of his art from the canon which never fully accepted black people in the first place, and simultaneously creating an avenue in

---

[5] Ytasha L. Womack, Afrofuturism: The World of Black Sci-Fi and Fantasy Culture (Chicago: Lawrence Hill Books, 2013) 109.
[6] Ytasha L. Womack, *Afrofuturism: The World of Black Sci-Fi and Fantasy Culture* (Chicago: Lawrence Hill Books, 2013) 63.

which black people could imagine a bright future for themselves through artistic representations. Afrofuturism itself is a widely debated and difficult to pin down idea with no agreed upon definition. As an artistic aesthetic, African-American artists are empowered to navigate the outer spaces of their imaginations to express their vision of the future and also re-conceive the past. Womack notes that the "cyclical nature of time" is a favorite theme for Afrofuturist artists to "redefine culture and notions of blackness for today and the future"[7] and that bi-directionality bridges the connections between past, present, and future.

One of the pioneers of the birth of hip hop and founder of the Universal Zulu Nation Afrika Bambaataa is one of many examples of Afrofuturist artists that were around well before the concept had a name. His legendary album *Planet Rock* (1986) is one of the earliest and most recognizable examples of Afrofuturism in hip hop. Public Enemy utilized the Afrofuturist aesthetic in the early 90s to deliver politically conscious albums like *Fear of a Black Planet* (1990) and *Apocalypse 91… The Enemy Strikes Black* (1991). It is important to point out that Outkast started their career around the same time that Afrofuturism gained a foothold in African-American critical studies, putting out their Afrofuturist masterpiece *ATLiens* in 1996 and its follow up *Aquemini* in 1998. Pharrell Williams and Chad Hugo started an Afrofutuist record label in 2001 named Star Trak Entertainment and Lil' Wayne developed an alien persona throughout the 2000s ultimately releasing *I Am Not a Human Being* in 2010. Although these artists (and many more) should not be universally labeled as strictly Afrofuturist artists, it is undeniable that they have all found comfort and effectiveness in delivering their artistic message through the aesthetic of Afrofuturism, often fluctuating between abandoning it all together and exclusively using it to produce their music and send a futuristic message.

Kendrick Lamar is one of these artists. His 2015 album *To Pimp a Butterfly* was undeniably successful, being named top album of the year by multiple publications and being nominated for 11 Grammys,

---

[7] Ytasha L. Womack, Afrofuturism: The World of Black Sci-Fi and Fantasy Culture (Chicago: Lawrence Hill Books, 2013) 153, 9.

including Album of the Year. Kendrick relies on multiple tropes of Afrofuturist art on the album, including, but not limited to, time and space travel, multi-ego, and alien persona in order to express personal and cultural turmoil related to being African-American in the new millennium, during mass incarceration of a disproportionate number of black individuals, systematic racial oppression and underrepresentation in government, and the Black Lives Matter movement motivated by police brutality of black individuals.

2.

Kendrick Lamar: The Pimp or the Butterfly?

Before trying to decipher the potential intention, meaning, and/or message of *To Pimp a Butterfly*, we must understand some background of who Kendrick Lamar is, and what from his past might have helped shape his artistic vision. Obviously, some works of art can standalone as important pieces, their intention untainted or changed by the background of the artist. Some literary, art, or cultural critics prefer to separate the art from the artist in question in order to offer an unbiased opinion, critique, or assessment of the work. This is not one of those projects. Not only is Kendrick Lamar becoming too big a star in the music world for a critic not to know anything about his personal life or beliefs, but his personal history and background are relevant to consider when looking at *To Pimp a Butterfly* as an artist's expression in historical, political, and personal context.

Kendrick Lamar Duckworth was born in June of 1987, in Compton, California, a city which serves as the central geographical focal point of most of his work, as well as the unofficial capital of West coast hip hop. Originally from Chicago, Illinois, Kendrick's parents moved west reportedly to escape some trouble that Kendrick's father was in on the rough streets of Chicago. Lamar relates, "They were going to go to San Bernardino, but my Auntie Tina was in Compton. She got 'em a hotel until they got on their feet, and my mom got a job at McDonald's. For the first couple of years, they slept in their car or motels, or in the park when it was hot enough. Eventually, they saved enough money to get their first apartment, and that's when they had me."[8]

Growing up poor, in a city where gang rivalries and crime were an almost everyday occurrence, Kendrick was shaped by both the music around him and the hard truths of the streets. Named after The

---

[8] Qtd. In Josh Ellis, "The Trials of Kendrick Lamar," *Rolling Stone*, June 22, 2015.

Temptations singer Eddie Kendricks, Lamar (like many African-American youth) grew up listening to the soul, R&B, and funk of their parent's generation, mixed with the gangsta rap of the streets of Compton in the 90s, when N.W.A., Snoop Doggy Dogg, and Tupac Shakur dominated West coast hip hop. Like many of Compton's youth, Kendrick recalls being tempted into troublesome behavior has a young man, but ultimately music usurped the temptation of the street life, and at a young age, Kendrick was coming into his own as a talented hip hop artist.

When Kendrick was 16 years old, he released his first-full length project, under the pseudonym K-Dot, titled *Youngest Head Nigga in Charge* in 2003. Two years later, his 26-track mixtape *Training Day* started to gain him attention amongst hip hop's biggest names including one of the most prolific and celebrated rappers on the 2000s Lil' Wayne. Wayne co-signed Lamar and released his third mixtape in 2009 titled *C4*, which Lamar modeled after Lil' Wayne's extremely successful album *Tha Carter III*. Kendrick, who decided to drop the moniker K-Dot and go by his given name Kendrick Lamar, dropped a self-titled EP later in 2009, beginning the process of transforming from a mixtape artist into a rapper who began putting out proper records. Inspired and mentored by Lil' Wayne, Kendrick identified with the rapper who was short in stature (both are 5'5") but gigantic in charisma and rhyming ability. Wayne, an Afrofuturist rapper who takes on multiple personas, using changing vocal characteristics and an often alien persona, offers quick witted and unfatigued lyrics that have become a staple of Kendrick's style. Although Kendrick has developed a lyrical style and flow that is now all his own, it is easy to see Lil' Wayne's influence in all of his records.

Kendrick, still an independent artist, made the leap to full-length and fully realized album when he released *Section.80* in July of 2011. The album received critical acclaim and lead to Kendrick being signed by Interscope Records and Dr. Dre's (another rapper born in Compton, California) Aftermath Entertainment in March of 2012. The title *Section.80* is a play on government subsidized section 8 housing projects, and how Kendrick's generation was born in the 80s, where Reaganomics and conservative political agendas, such as the war on drugs and the policies of the Justice Department's Civil Rights division, obstructed the enforcement of civil rights laws and continuously oppressed and hindered the advancement of African-American's social status in an already racially unequal America. For Kendrick to place himself within this political and historical context as a young hip hop artist, showed he was fully prepared to establish himself outside of hip hop's popular materialistic culture, and instead partake in a more involved and in-depth look at African-American culture and the treatment of black people in American society, a path he has continued to take as his career has developed.

Kendrick's major-label debut, *good kid, m.A.A.d city* was released on October 22, 2012. Again, Kendrick's work received critical acclaim, and now with greater distribution that reached a larger audience, it debuted as the number two selling album in the country selling 242,100 copies in its first week. Nine months after its release, *good kid, m.A.A.d city* was certified platinum and earned seven Grammy nominations including one for Album of the Year at the 56th Grammy Awards. The concept of the album follows a Joycean day in the life of Kendrick as a teenager in Compton, often allured by the temptations of the streets, but ultimately *good kid, m.A.A.d city* is an ode to his hometown and a stark look at what it is like to grow up a black man in America. The album was included on hundreds of publication's year-end lists, holding the top spot on many of them. A world tour followed, and Kendrick Lamar's place as one of the most talented, sought after, and celebrated hip hop artists was secured.

It took two and a half years for *good kid, m.A.A.d city*'s follow-up to be released. Not only was Kendrick touring consistently off the success of the album with fellow members of the hip hop collective Black Hippy, but also as support for Kanye West. According to Engineer/Mixer Derek "MixedByAll" Ali, a tour stop in South Africa, "led Lamar to scrap 'two or three albums worth of material.'"[9] Clearly

Kendrick was working tirelessly on a plethora of material for a new album[10] but the trip to South Africa allowed him to come up with the concept of his third LP, and the focus of this work led to the release of *To Pimp a Butterfly* on March 15th, 2015. Kendrick found himself on top of the U.S. Billboard chart, besting *good kid, m.A.A.d city* and selling 324,000 copies in the first week, while also breaking the single day streaming record on Spotify by being played 9.6 million times. Like *good kid, m.A.A.d city*, *To Pimp a Butterfly* landed on hundreds of year-end lists, topping many of them as the Album of the Year. It also earned him two Grammy wins at the 57th Grammy Awards, and eleven Grammy nominations at the 58th Grammy Awards, again including Album of the Year, and resulting in five more Grammy wins. Of the album, Kendrick says, "I wanted to do a record like this on my debut album but I wasn't confident enough,"[11] and as this project wishes to show, *To Pimp A Butterfly* is as creative as it is personal, as ambitious as it is game-changing, and as futuristic as it is rooted in who Kendrick Lamar is as a person, through his childhood and the ancestry of his family.

Conscious Rap Background

Rap/Hip Hop as a genre was birthed out of a social consciousness that, although at times blinded by the reflection of an overpowering and loud "bling" culture, has been prevalent since Grandmaster Flash, DJ Kool Herc, and Afrika Bambaataa were first getting started in New York in the late 70s. Hip hop is a musical expression created by DJs who couldn't afford instruments or didn't have access to the lessons needed to learn how to play them, so instead

---

[9] Andreas Hale, "The Oral History of Kendrick Lamar's To Pimp a Butterfly," *The Grammys*. February 15, 2016.
[10] Many of the songs that were "scrapped" likely part of the eight tracks on Kendrick's 2016 release *untitled unmastered*.
[11] Andreas Hale, "The Oral History of Kendrick Lamar's To Pimp a Butterfly," The Grammys. February 15, 2016.

they made the most of what they had, learning how to sample and splice breakbeats and scratch records on a pair of turntables allowing them to reimagine the music they were influenced by, while creating their own expressive creative output. Suddenly, the musical possibilities for these music producers was endless as they could potentially and quite literally pull from the entirety of musical history to make the sonic backdrop to which MCs would rap over. Likewise, these MCs used nothing but their voices, whether smooth, rough, rugged, raw, or flowing to become storytellers, braggadocios, social commentators, villains, heroes, or any possible character or persona they liked. The combinations of these infinite possibilities created by DJs and MCs working together was apparent at the beginning of hip hop, and that tradition has remained, although often expanded, to the music we still hear today.

Although conscious rap was a staple of the genre's inception, it wasn't until the late 80s and early 90s that socially charged rap was truly placed at the forefront of the genre and given a "prominent mainstream platform" for which the artists could express social issues addressed in the music to a national audience. As Collin Robinson of the music website Stereogum claims of the time period, it was "arguably an even more tumultuous time for black America, with crack wreaking havoc on top of police brutality. Public Enemy and N.W.A.[12] responded in kind with candid imagery, but their shock value has worn off with time."[13] Maybe the shock value of politically charged albums from those groups have worn off, either due to the realization that it is now the past and not part of our present, that we are aware of the racial tensions and systemic oppression of the black community still prevailing from Reagan-era policies, or we have become desensitized by the gangsta rap that used to be shocking but no longer is because it has been a part of our cultural lives for 30 years. Whatever the reason, it is clear that when racial tensions, although always prevalent in American

---

[12] See also A Tribe Called Quest and KRS-One.
[13] Collin Robinson, "Kendrick Lamar And Mainstream Rap's Growing Conscience," *Stereogum*, January 5, 2016.

society, are reaching a peaking point, that a new wave of socially conscious hip hop artists emerge and begin to creatively take over the genre.

As hip hop's popularity continued to grow, becoming the soundtrack to many urban African-American communities, and spreading across the nation and the world, a new group of socially conscious rappers rose to popularity in the mid to late 90s. As a response to almost a decade of gangsta rap dominance, it was becoming clear that the social messages of gangsta rap's early years was giving way to the materialist and radio friendly sound of the "bling era". "Cash Money, Bad Boy, Death Row, and No Limit dominated the radio, moved millions of units, and became the public face of rap,"[14] while a new wave of conscience rap emerged with artists like Talib Kweli, the Roots, Mos Def, Dead Prez, Nas, Aesop Rock, Atmosphere, Tupac Shakur and many others. Although many of these artists continue to put out politically charged hip hop today, another wave of conscience rappers has emerged alongside the Black Lives Matter Movement, including Kendrick Lamar. Some have called for people to stop using the term "conscience rap" indicating that all hip hop, and art for that matter, is in some ways conscience and at least reflective of culture and society, but it seems a useful term in terms of discussing artists, songs, or albums that are purposefully and overtly socially conscience in response to a particular problem, issue, or event within society.

That being said, Kendrick seems to be an artist that doesn't believe in being socially aware, but simply in being. He says, "A lot of y'all don't understand Kendrick Lamar because you wonder how I can talk about money, hoes, clothes, God, and history all in the same sentence. […] I'm not on the outside looking in. I'm not on the inside looking out. I'm in the dead fucking center, looking around… I'm not the next pop star. I'm not the next socially aware rapper. I am a human motherfucking being over dope-ass instrumentation."[15] Kendrick is not

---

[14] Collin Robinson, "Kendrick Lamar And Mainstream Rap's Growing Conscience," Stereogum, January 5, 2016.
[15] Collin Robinson, "Kendrick Lamar And Mainstream Rap's Growing

socially aware; he is a part of society. His music is not a cultural commentary; it is culture.

Critical Reception of Conscious Rap

Out of 145 individual year-end lists compiled by the website Metacritic, Kendrick Lamar's *To Pimp a Butterfly* appeared on 101 of those lists, holding the top spot for Album of the Year on 51 of those lists, earning it Metacritic's 4th "Best Music and Albums of All-Time". Of course, this is a statistical analysis of music critics and publications and doesn't necessarily directly correlate to the arbitrary title of the best of all-time. However, as shown, the acclaim of *To Pimp a Butterfly* undeniably places it, at the very least, as one of the most critically celebrated albums of its time. The list of influential publications that proclaimed *To Pimp a Butterfly* as the Best Album of the Year is staggering and unheard of, including Billboard, Complex, Consequence of Sound, Entertainment Weekly, Pitchfork Media, Rolling Stone, SPIN, The Guardian, and Vice. As many of the reviews indicate, this critical acclimation is not limited to praising it as a successful piece of hip hop music, but moreover as an influential and necessary social statement, rooted within the current volatile racial atmosphere of America.

After receiving a total of seven Grammy nominations (but winning zero) for *good kid, m.A.A.d city* in 2014 at the 56th Annual Grammy Awards, Kendrick was awarded two Grammy wins in 2015 for Best Rap Song and Best Rap Performance for the *To Pimp a Butterfly* single "i", a joyful ode to self-love. In 2016, Kendrick was nominated for eleven Grammys prior to the release of the entire *To Pimp a Butterfly* album, one nomination shy of Michael Jackson's record and breaking Eminem's record for most nominations by a rapper. The whitewashed awards panel awarded Kendrick five Grammys, specifically within the genre category of rap, choosing to give Album of the Year awards to the non-controversial or political pop star Taylor Swift, a decision that

---

Conscience," Stereogum, January 5, 2016.

ultimately did not come to the surprise of anyone who understands race and white privilege in America, but was still puzzling to consider when placing the two albums' social and artistic contributions side-by-side.[16]

Kendrick Lamar's performance at the 58th Grammy Award ceremony goes further to expose how frightening a powerful and politically charged young voice from Compton can be to the social sensibilities of white America. Kendrick appeared in a line of black men, dressed as a prisoner in chains frantically rapping "The Blacker the Berry" until stumbling over to another part of the stage, where a fire raged behind him as he rapped the Black Lives Matter anthem "Alright". The performance was intoxicating and aggressive; a commentary on the mass incarceration of young black men, and the riotous frustration the black community feels about police brutality and the lack of justice for the individuals in power who murder unarmed black citizens. What was most telling (and probably goes a long way to explain how Taylor Swift upset Kendrick for Album of the Year), was the brief camera cuts to the mostly white individuals in the audience who looked confused, shocked, and frightened of the artist on stage. For much of the audience, both at the Grammys and watching at home, the performance was a rude awakening of the increased racial tensions and cultural frustrations within the black community, and by awarding *To Pimp a Butterfly* its deserved Album of the Year title, the Grammys would have reinforced the social magnitude of Kendrick's message, something they clearly were not ready or willing to do.

Awards aside, *To Pimp a Butterfly* will still go down as one of the most celebrated and socially conscious albums of our time. Billboard argues that, "twenty years ago, a conscious rap record wouldn't have penetrated the mainstream in the way Kendrick Lamar did with *To Pimp a Butterfly* […] His sense of timing is impeccable. In the midst of rampant cases of police brutality and racial tension across America, he spews raw, aggressive bars while possibly cutting a rug."[17]

---

[16] See also the 59th Grammy Awards when Adele beat out the universally critically acclaimed Beyoncé album *Lemonade*, causing Adele to admit she didn't deserve the award and Beyoncé did.

This assessment implies both that progress is being made in allowing black rappers to express their frustrations with society to a broader audience, and that the issues of racial inequalities and tensions are more prevalent in America's civil consciousness than twenty years ago because of artists and performers like Kendrick Lamar who refuse to be pigeonholed in the purview of a politically correct national conversation. This nod towards the past but projection into the future is exactly what *To Pimp a Butterfly* accomplishes so well. The New York Times' Jon Pereles placed *To Pimp a Butterfly* as the Best Album of the Year stating, "It's an immensely musical album: a dense caldron of funk, jazz and soul that draws hope and determination from the past, confronting problems that past eras have left unsolved."[18] Not much has changed in regard to racism since the Civil Rights Movement. We are still a racist nation, built on racism, and with many racist people, but the future is now as far as what needs to be done to solve some of the systematic policies and attitudes keeping people of color oppressed. SPIN Magazine dubbed *To Pimp a Butterfly* the "Great American Hip-Hop Album" not only alluding to the importance of it as an enduring portrait of our times, but as a culturally defining piece of art that enhances, inspires, and motivates society to be better.[19]

The success and overall message of *To Pimp a Butterfly* has led to not only recognition from cultural critics, but from political figures that see his artistic vision as helpful to the community. Kendrick was given the key to the City of Compton by Mayor Aja Brown on February 13th, 2016 and was named a Generational Icon by the California Senate in May of 2015.[20] Both acknowledgements mean a great deal as a

---

[17] "Billboard.com's 25 Best Albums of 2015: Critics' Picks." *Billboard*, December 15, 2015.
[18] Jon Pareles, "The Best Albums of 2015," *The New York Times*, December 9, 2015.
[19] Dan Weiss, "Review: Kendrick Lamar Returns With the Great American Hip-Hop Album, 'To Pimp a Butterfly'," *SPIN*, March 20, 2015.
[20] Althea Legaspi, "Kendrick Lamar to Receive Key to Compton," *Rolling Stone*, January 14, 2016.

socially conscious rapper is credited for being a positive role model in California, a drastic change to the challenges gangster rappers faced in the 90s when politicians pushed to have their music censored and banned from the airwaves. As we will later discuss in further detail, Kendrick's relationship with the City of Compton and the West coast runs deep, as he acknowledges and struggles with the responsibility of being a spokesperson as well as a role model. Kendrick said of these honors, "There's a lot of kids that grew up the way I did, that feel like there's no way out. We don't get a lot of celebrities or whatnot to come to the city and actually put they hand back in the city and say, 'You can do it, too.' I feel like it's only right that I champion them, let them know I'll always be behind them. Let them know I know the sacrifices and the struggles they go through and give 'em some type of inspiration."[21] For underprivileged children in Compton, to see a positive strong celebrity role model vow to stand up for them in the face of gang violence and criminal pressures is an important an uncommon message for them to receive. That is what Kendrick Lamar uses his art for, to spread a positive message throughout his community in contrast to what the media or society might tell those kids. This is why Kendrick has been championed by both politicians in the community and by President Obama on a national level, because he strives to make a positive difference through his art, and is unafraid, unapologetic, and unwilling to be compromised.

---

[21] Victoria Hernadez, "Kendrick Lamar Receives Key To The City of Compton, California," *Hip Hop DX*, February 13, 2016.

To Pimp a Butterfly: How *To Pimp a Butterfly* Tackles the Music (Rap) Industry

[Kendrick Lamar]

Aight so let me ask you this then, do you see yourself as somebody that's rich or somebody that made the best of their own opportunities?

[Tupac Shakur]

I see myself as a natural born hustler, a true hustler in every sense of the word. I took nothin', I took the opportunities, I worked at the most menial and degrading job and built myself up so I could get it to where I owned it. I went from having somebody manage me to me hiring the person that works my management company. I changed everything, I realized my destiny in a matter of five years you know what I'm saying I made myself a millionaire. I made millions for a lot of people now it's time to make millions for myself, you know what I'm saying. I made millions for the record companies, I made millions for these movie companies, now I make millions for us.[22]

Kendrick Lamar is not shy about sending a message to the rap music industry, claiming to be the current king of hip hop and consciously raising the bar with *To Pimp a Butterfly*'s creativity, socio-political message, and album sales, a trio of elements that no one of this era can yet challenge. However, the claim to being the king of hip hop is something that is often seen in an industry that champions boastful lyrics. In *To Pimp a Butterfly*, Kendrick goes further to examine and critique not only the rap industry, but the entirety of the music industry,

---

[22] "Mortal Man"

specifically how it treats black artists. Not only does he metaphorically portray the industry as the devil (Lucy) and a girlfriend from a destructive relationship, but he connects the current landscape of being an African-American in the music industry to slavery. As the self-proclaimed king of one of the most popular and important genres of African-American music, Kendrick is in a position to not only be critical of the history of how black artists before him have been treated, but also to challenge the status quo of the industry that has cheated artists out of the monetary compensation they have deserved for decades.

On the opening track "Wesley's Theory," Kendrick introduces a common analogy in hip hop where he personifies the rap industry as a woman he is in a relationship with. Multiple examples of this analogy can be found in the history of hip hop, both as a positive metaphor in which the artist loves or is dedicated to the "game" and the craft of writing rhymes, and also as a negative representation in which the relationship to the game is a destructive one that the artist finds difficult to escape. Similarly, many rappers have personified gang life (also known as the "game") as a woman that they love and are dedicated to but cannot escape in the face of societal capitalist pressures. Since Kendrick was able to avoid the gang life that surrounded him in Compton, the "game" represents the music industry.

In "Wesley's Theory" the industry is Kendrick's "first girlfriend", someone who he was introduced to at a young age and who he loved. He raps, "at first, I did love you/but now I just wanna fuck" indicating that when he was first introduced to the game, he was infatuated and in love, but as he has grown up and learned more about how the industry treats its artists and uses them only to its advantage, not caring about them as people or artists, he now only wants to fuck, either using the industry to his own artistic advantage or to fuck up the industry by stirring the pot and changing how the game is played. In the first verse of "Wesley's Theory," Kendrick plays the role of his naïve younger self, an excited and materialistic young rapper who is fascinated and motivated by the amount of money he can make. He raps of "platinum on everythin', platinum on weddin' ring/married to the game and a bad bitch chose" in which his puppy love for the game leads him not only to want to give it a platinum wedding ring, but also have platinum on everything, or more specifically have his records go platinum as a result of his dedication to the game.

The title of the track "Wesley's Theory" is an allusion to actor Wesley Snipes who, despite being in over 100 movies, was charged with tax fraud and sentenced to three years in prison for failing to file his federal tax return.[23] The idea that a wealthy African-American celebrity can get in financial trouble is something that Kendrick is wary of.[24] Kendrick knows, that if he isn't careful, the rap industry is going to pimp him, make money off him, and leave him in the lurch if he fails to manage his finances or gets into trouble with the U.S. government, whether it be tax/money related or if charged with a crime. Being conscientious of this means that Kendrick's stint with naïveté as it relates to the music industry is short lived and his present understanding of the evils of the rap industry is a theme throughout *To Pimp a Butterfly*.

In "You Ain't Gotta Lie (Momma Said)", Kendrick critiques the moral absolutism that celebrities, and particularly black celebrities, are held to. Similar to alluding to Wesley Snipes' tax problems, Kendrick addresses Michael Jackson's alleged child molestation saying "that nigga gave us Billie Jean, you say he touched those kids?/when shit hit the fan, is you still a fan?" Two other overarching themes of *To Pimp a Butterfly* are forgiveness and how American culture finds a sadistic joy in seeing celebrities fail. Here, Kendrick is not speculating on whether or not Michael Jackson in fact molested children. He is not here to judge a man or condemn him for his flaws. As Tupac Shakur said "only God can judge me," but like Tupac, Kendrick idolizes Michael Jackson as a revolutionary artist that positively influenced millions of fans and generations of artists. The media, the industry, and a large part of society are ready to write-off a celebrity that has any sort of controversy

---

[23] Ann Oldenburg, "Wesley Snipes finishes prison time for tax evasion," *USA Today*, April 5, 2013.
[24] See also Mike Tyson.

or problem, where Kendrick sees that forgiveness is the key, not only for celebrities, but for all people. The industry is not your friend and will likely benefit as much from your failure as it will by your success. By using these examples of beloved artists whose legacies have been tainted, Kendrick understands that he has to be careful to not allow the industry to pimp him and make him its own. He must stand firm in his own artistry and allow his heart to decide where his career and personal path take him.

As we will see, Lucy represents the personification of a lot of negative and destructive things that Kendrick grapples with in *To Pimp a Butterfly*. Lucy, a clear nickname for Lucifer, is the feminism temptress and the main antagonist in Kendrick's self-exploration as he battles her in the spiritual realm. On the track "For Sale (Interlude)" Kendrick raps, "then you spit a little rap to me like this/when I turned 26 I was like 'oh shit'/you said to me/I remember what you said too, you said/'My name is Lucy, Kendrick/You introduced me Kendrick'" and although Kendrick was involved in the rap game well before he was 26-years-old, that is the age that his debut album *Section.80* was released and he was truly introduced to the industry. Kendrick also alludes to the TV show "I Love Lucy", further connecting the temptations of the devil to the entertainment industry.

How the current landscape of the music industry is portrayed is constantly being compared to slavery in *To Pimp a Butterfly*. Record executives using black artists as vessels of profitability has been part of the history of music in America for nearly a century. Track titles like "For Free? (Interlude)" and "For Sale? (Interlude)," along with Kendrick's powerful proclamation "this dick ain't free" places *To Pimp a Butterfly* as a record that is not going to fall in line with the history of black music being marginalized and used for the financial benefit of people in power who did little to support the conception of the album. On "You Ain't Gotta Lie (Momma Said)", Kendrick (personifying his mother) reiterates what he has been struggling with for much of the album when he raps "circus acts only attract those that entertain/small talk, we know that it's all talk". Kendrick refuses to be a circus act, only placed in the public eye to entertain, or a pawn for the record industry. He goes on to say, "and sell a dream in the auction, tell me just who your boss is" not only comparing being a music artist and having your art auctioned off to slavery, but reiterating that artists are not their own bosses and are slaves to the money-making aims of the industry.[25] In saying "study long, study wrong", Kendrick understands that studying the past of African-American artists who were pimped by the industry and potentially repeating their careers will not help him in his own, but that through his own self-discovery and experience, he can break free from the pressures and mistakes of his predecessors.

Kendrick, being proclaimed "King" of hip hop by legends of the game[26], refuses to let the industry pimp him and dictate who he is as an artist. In "King Kunta" Kendrick stands firm in his authenticity in the face of the materialistic and commercial "bling" culture in hip hop as he raps, "and if I gotta brown nose for some gold/then I'd rather be a bum than a motherfuckin' baller". Kendrick would rather be penniless and unknown than to suck up to the powers that be. Likewise, during the first verse of "Alright", Kendrick reiterates that despite what the industry wants from him, he will only rap for himself and his community and not for the industry's economic or political purposes. Kendrick seems sick of the hypocrisy of the industry as he raps in "Hood Politics", "critics want to mention that they miss when hip hop was rappin'/motherfucker, if you did, then Killer Mike'd be platinum" paying homage to another conscience rapper Killer Mike, who raps about political issues and is a true black activist speaking up for the African-American community. Kendrick knows that being political or real doesn't equate to being successful in the rap game, but as the King of hip hop, he is in a place where he can challenge that conception and hopefully lead the future of hip hop into a new era. In "i" he raps, "peace to fashion police, I wear my heart/on my sleeve, let the runway start" and in the video for the track he is seen running down the street

---

[25] See also Kanye West's "New Slaves".
[26] Jeff Weiss, "Snoop Dogg, Dr. Dre and Game pass torch to Kendrick Lamar," *Los Angeles Times*, August 24, 2011.

in simple fashion, wearing a plain white t-shirt and a baseball cap with no logo. This is yet another example that Kendrick refuses to let the industry dictate who he is as an artist. His "fashion" is wearing his heart on his sleeve and as "let the runway start" simultaneously alludes to a fashion runway and runaway slaves, Kendrick is leading the industry away from current industry expectations and into a future where the artists are the dictators and not the slaves of the industry.

3.

Multi-Ego: Multi-Consciousness and the Many Personas of Kendrick Lamar

As we see more and more throughout art history, individual artists adopt different personas or aesthetics of self to support their artistic vision. Some cultural and art critics insist on separating the artist from the work of art so as not to detract or distract from the analysis of the piece itself. However, the more we see artists reinvent their own persona while reinventing or simply producing a new piece of art, the more the artist themselves become relevant to the overall presentation and production of the work. Possibly more than any other artistic medium, the reinvention or representation of self is extremely prevalent in music. Artists, like the recently deceased David Bowie and Prince, often reinvent their image to coincide with a new chapter in their musical careers in order to supplement their next album release. Although always staying true to himself, Bob Dylan adopted various personas throughout his career. We grow as people throughout our lives. Some changes of persona are small, and some are groundbreaking. For some musicians, taking creative license with the persona they put out into the world can be as important as their creative musical output.

Hip hop is one of the music genres we often see the adoption of alter-egos. It is almost impossible to find a hip hop artists that chooses to rap under their given birth name. Even Tupac Shakur adopted the alias 2Pac on his album covers. This reinvention allows hip hop artists to be even more confident, aggressive, or make claims to events or personal beliefs that do not necessarily line up with their life history or feelings. Alter-egos allow artists to adopt the role of both storyteller and character(s) within the story being told and they allow artists to separate their art from their self, and thus explore the inner workings of that self from an outside perspective.

Hip hop artists in particular often take on multiple personas within a song, an album, and a career, creating what Kodwo Eshun calls "multi-egos".[27] In his groundbreaking conceptual book that addresses Afrofuturist music *More Brilliant Than The Sun: Adventures in Sonic Fiction*, Eshun introduces the concept of the multi-ego using the example of hip hop artist Kool Keith who, born Keith Thornton, goes by many aliases including Dr. Octagon, Dr. Doom, Black Elvis, Dr. Ultra, Poppa Large, Rhythm X, Funk Igniter Plus, and Crazy Lou. This is far from uncommon in the hip hop world as most rappers refer to themselves by various nicknames other than the one that they put on the album cover. Eshun asserts that "I is a crowd" and that by assuming these various personas, Kool Keith empowers himself and his work by allowing freedom and wiggle room to explore various modes of self. Eshun writes that "instead of putting the scientific self back together or mending the broken fragments of the cybernetic psyche, Kool Keith heightens what used to be called schizophrenia, intensifies the crackup and the breakdown. The self doesn't split up or multiply into heteronyms. Rather, the self no longer amputates itself down to a single part but it instead asserts that I is a crowd, that the human is a population of processes."[28] These processes can be extracted, melded, dismissed, embraced, and/or subsequently used as an internal tool of self-examination or an external tool of examination of the world around us.

For Eshun, the names and personas that rappers/musicians adopt are not fake but heteronymous or "a many-name, one in a series of parallel names which distributes and disperses you into the public secrecy of open anonymity. [...] Alter-egos are more real because you choose them. Ordinary names are unreal because you didn't. Multi-egos are more real still because they designate your parallel states."[29] Reminiscent of W.E.B. du Bois' idea of double consciousness, the multi-consciousness that hip hop artists use allows them to broaden the application and usage of language to approach different issues of self,

---

[27] Kodwo, Eshun, *More Brilliant Than The Sun: Adventures In Sonic Fiction* (London, England: Quartet Books, 1998). 27.
[28] Kodwo, Eshun, *More Brilliant Than The Sun: Adventures In Sonic Fiction* (London, England: Quartet Books, 1998). 26-27.
[29] Ibid, 106.

community, culture, and society from different, ever-changing, and unique angles. Eshun believes that artists like Kool Keith flip the script on often demeaning or destructive psychological disorders when he writes, "multiple personality is no syndrome or disorder but a relaxation, a giving into rather than a fighting against the brain as a *society* of mind" (Eshun's emphasis).[30]

In *To Pimp a Butterfly*, Kendrick Lamar (born Kendrick Duckworth), utilizes this concept to his powerful advantage as he creates a multi-ego crowd in order to explore the deepest caverns of his depression to the hopeful and positive vision he sees possible for, not only the African-American community but, America as a whole. Kendrick's multi-ego shows itself in a variety of ways. First, Kendrick's depression is negative and internalized throughout the album. He time travels within his own psyche to revisit his younger self as a source of pride and accomplish for what he has learned throughout the journey he has taken. He adopts the roles of multiple characters in order to speak for the African-American community, examining the pressures he faces externally as a role model, spokesperson, and anointed King of Hip Hop, and also in sending a positive message of hope and faith out into the community. He takes on a religious role like that of a preacher in order to examine the same external pressures, but also to utilize the internal guidance which allows him to accept his role and stay faithful to that which is true and right. Finally, he embodies the Devil (Lucy) and the personification of America to assess the pressure of sin and what is expected, not only of himself as a black man, but of all the citizens of the United States and what their role is in uplifting and supporting each other. This chapter will explore how each of these transformations of self are used in *To Pimp a Butterfly* and how/why Kendrick is able to artistically cover so much substantially critical ground by utilizing the multi-ego concept. The self acts as a multi-ego, just as a community and a society acts as a multi-ego. "I is a crowd."

---

[30] Ibid, 27.

The Negative Internalization of Depression

Throughout *To Pimp a Butterfly* Kendrick Lamar faces many obstacles, both internally and externally, on his journey of self-examination and for understanding where he has come from, where he is currently at in his career, and where he is going. One of the more prominent and intimate struggles he introduces is his struggle with depression, presumably reaching a tipping point in a hotel room when Kendrick was on the Yeezus tour with Kanye West in 2014.[31] Kendrick utilizes the concept of multi-ego in order to assess his struggle with depression by having internalized conversations about what in his life he believes is the source of the depression, what he thinks about himself and his actions, and how he handles the pressures of fame, family, friendship, and being a role model on top off the rap game. As a genre often reliant on boastfulness personalities that champion mental strength and confidence, hip hop does not exactly invite artists to dwell on their struggles with mental illness. That is not to say that rappers completely avoid the subject. Many lyricists over the years have taken opportunities to address dealing with depression in certain verses or songs, but it is rare for an artist to intimately grapple with depression for nearly an entire album. Tupac Shakur comes to mind when looking back on the history of hip hop artists that, through their music, allowed the listener into deep, and often dark, depths of their psyche.

Kendrick begins to let the listener into his struggles with depression on the song "Institutionalized" and the revenge plot of "These Walls". "Institutionalized" serves as a double meaning that connects two of the major themes of *To Pimp a Butterfly*; Kendrick's mental health issues and how the African-American community has been institutionally suppressed since slavery by various government policies, mass imprisonment of African-Americans, and systematic racism. Connecting these two themes in one track, Kendrick is possibly hinting that one of the reasons that he is depressed, or that many subjugated people in America today are depressed, and "belong in a

---

[31] Dorian Lynskey, "Kendrick Lamar: 'I am Trayvon Martin. I'm all of these kids'," *The Guardian*. June 21, 2015.

mental institution" is because they feel trapped in a society where they can't advance themselves or their community. Guilt plays a formative role in Kendrick's depression and the guilt of not being able to help the people in his community that are struggling only exacerbates his internal struggles. In the next track "These Walls", Kendrick seeks revenge from a man who is in prison for killing Kendrick's friend, by sleeping with the man's woman while he is locked up. Kendrick ultimately finds no satisfaction in the act of revenge, but instead finds himself turning to depression and self-hate as he contemplates suicide in a hotel room during the track "u".

"u" serves as the pinnacle of Kendrick's battle with depression and is in direct contrast to *To Pimp a Butterfly*'s lead single "i", which is an anthem that pronounces self-love and positivity for Kendrick and the African-American community. However, in "u", Kendrick battles with the negative thoughts that plague his mind, looking deep into his soul to examine mistakes he has made in his personal life and how fame has affected him professionally. At one point during the track, Kendrick refers to himself as "a fucking failure" blurring the line between his professional and personal lives, since he is not a professional failure in the eyes of critics, media, or fans, something is plaguing Kendrick as he screams in the hotel room at the end of "These Walls", causing him to contemplate suicide.[32]

Of the track, Kendrick has said, "that was one of the hardest songs I had to write. There's some very dark moments in there. All my insecurities and selfishness and let-downs. That shit is depressing as a motherfucker. But it helps, though. It helps."[33] Not only is it a rare occurrence for a rapper at the top of the game to admit mental illness and personal struggles, but his use of the word "had" when he says, "one of the hardest song I *had* to write" is telling as if "u" was the track that allowed the rest of the project to formulate. A journey of the

---

[32] Dorian Lynskey, "Kendrick Lamar: 'I am Trayvon Martin. I'm all of these kids'," *The Guardian*. June 21, 2015.
[33] Josh Ellis, "The Trials of Kendrick Lamar," *Rolling Stone*, June 22, 2015.

discovery of self-love is not complete without the protagonist reaching the rock-bottom point of his soul, and "u" is Kendrick reaching that bottom.

On the track, we find Kendrick at an all-time emotional low caused by pressure from critics and fans who say he is the savior of hip hop, as well as the guilt he feels because his career, and traveling around the world, has taken him away from his family and home. Kendrick's younger sister became pregnant while he was away, and in the first verse of "u" Kendrick bemoans not being a more positive influence on her life. As one of the most influential rap artists in the world, Kendrick can have positive and life-changing influences on his fans while his career distracts him from the true importance of his family and personal guilt mounts. He raps, "situations, I'll start with your little sister bakin'/a baby inside, just a teenager, where your patience?/where was your antennas, where was the influence you speak of?/you preached in front of 100,000 but never reached her." In these bars, Kendrick plays the role of his conscience blaming himself for not being a stronger influence in his sister's life. It is interesting to note that he also views himself as a preacher to the fans that listen to him, a role he adopts throughout the album, but also points out that his "antennas" aren't picking up the more important things he should be paying attention to regarding his personal relationships. Kendrick unfairly imagines (or hopes) that he possesses these science fiction-like antennas, the extra sensing power of an insect (or alien?), of which he can submit and read radio waves telling him that his family is in trouble and he must help them. This analogous assessment is harsh and ultimately unfair, but Kendrick feels the guilt nonetheless because he does not possess this superhuman power as he calls himself a "fuckin' failure" and "no leader".

Kendrick re-introduces his problems with alcoholism[34] in the bridge of the track but this is only a temporary and fleeting numbing of the rooted depression within. We continue to find Kendrick breaking

---

[34] See "Swimming Pools (Drank)" from *good kid, m.A.A.d city.*

down in the hotel room as the quality of sound begins to break, symbolizing his emotional state and leading into a skit scene where a Spanish maid knocks on his hotel room door to clean his room. The Afrofuturist elements permeate this track as Kendrick is time travelling back to his lowest point and introducing the listener to a multi-ego faction of voices as he plays his guilty conscience, his drunken, manic, and emotionally unstable self, and what he believes are the criticisms against him within the hip hop community.

In the second verse of "u" Kendrick raps with a tearful delivery, mispronouncing words and muffling his voice to indicate his drunken state in the hotel room. He expresses concerns for leaving his hometown of Compton, while the city continues to struggle with crime, police brutality, and gang violence as he raps, "you ain't no brother, you ain't no disciple, you ain't no friend" touching on all aspects of responsibility that he feels towards his family, his fans, and the City of Compton. In an interview with GQ[35], Kendrick not only connects his sister's teenage pregnancy to his feeling of guilt, but also the death of his friend Chad who was killed in a drive-by shooting. Kendrick was overseas to promote his record while Chad was in the hospital, and Kendrick has said that he often feels guilty for FaceTiming his friend in the hospital, instead of coming home before he died.

In the third verse of "u", Kendrick's vocalized multi-ego again changes from angry scene in the hotel room, to a sadder and hurt voice that is once again from the perspective of his guilty conscience. His voice cracks and gulping sounds can be heard, indicating that Kendrick is still drinking, but instead of being angry in his guilt, Kendrick has now become depressed and contemplates suicide. He raps, "and if those mirrors could talk it would say 'you gotta go'/and if I told your secrets/the world'll know money can't stop a suicidal weakness". In contrast to "if these walls could talk", Kendrick has internalized his guilt and is looking at himself in the mirror to face his guilt and depression. The irony here is that his conscience is threatening to

---

[35] Steve Marsh, "Kendrick Lamar: Rapper of the Year," *GQ*. November 12, 2013.

expose Kendrick as depressed and suicidal, all while Kendrick himself is putting himself and his mental illness out into the world on the track.

A major aspect of Afrofuturist art is flipping the script on what Otherness means and instead making difference a powerful tool. For centuries labeling people or groups of people as Other has been a way in which to suppress the advancement of those people's civil rights and/or to justify treating them differently or with contempt. What Afrofuturism often does is make Otherness powerful. Blackness becomes a source of pride and difference becomes a superpower. Take the groundbreaking album *ATLiens* from Afrofuturist hip hop pioneers Outkast for example. Andre 3000 and Big Boi take on otherworldly and alien personas, giving them a superhuman aura found in science fiction comic books. The cover art of the *ATLiens* album is even modelled after the comic book aesthetic. Reverting to the founding analogy of Afrofuturism, that African-Americans were the first alien abductees taken from their homeland and enslaved on another planet, the idea that, as a people, those abductees were not only strong enough to survive in a foreign land, but to also find a place within society to thrive and prosper, is astonishing and commendable. To be alien is not only to be strong and resilient, but it is also to be cool and unique. In exposing his mental illness and guilty conscience to the world, Kendrick is risking an often-taboo showing of weakness in the hip hop community, but instead, in Otherizing himself within the hip hop world, he is in fact humanizing himself to the average listener. To be honest and to face your demons is to be powerful. In the drunken hotel room scene, Kendrick's "antennas" many not be catching all the waves he wishes they would, but in the crafting of "u", they are working efficiently regarding his self-understanding and discovery.

We can see the scene in the hotel room play out in Kendrick's "God Is Gangsta" music video where the opening shot finds Kendrick drinking liquor, drunk, sweaty, crawling around and yelling with frantic jazz playing in the background. The "God Is Gangsta" video is a medley of a few portions of *To Pimp a Butterfly* including parts of "u". Kendrick slumps in his chair, looking like he is about to vomit, spitting and yelling "lovin' you is complicated!" as he has seemingly hit rock bottom. He leans on the table in front of him, and the scene takes on a melty, psychedelic feel, as if the viewer is being transported through time with Kendrick who is remembering the scene. Kendrick frantically raps the first verse, seemingly to himself. As he stands up from the table, we see Kendrick's reflection in a mirror off to the side while the foggy drunk camera work jump cuts while he convulses, yells and raps, until everything slows down.

He raps the second verse looking straight into the camera, as if he is talking to himself in the reflection of the lens and is again frantically spitting and convulsing in disgust with himself. He holds a bottle of liquor while an empty bottle continuously spins on the table without stopping or slowing down, indicating (ala the film Inception) that this is a dream sequence based on the memory of the event, all while the image of Kendrick's reflection in the mirror appears and disappears. Kendrick's disconnection with reality and consciousness are visual representations of his growing depression while he was on tour with Kanye West. Of the time surrounding his breakdown in the hotel room, Kendrick said, "it was something that just accumulated. You know when you get bad news after bad news after bad news? And you can't express this to nobody but you got to relieve it in some type of way? I was able to bottle that moment and put in on record,"[36] and he has admitted that the pressures of fame and having many people look up to him exacerbated his negative feelings. Kendrick, disappearing and reappearing in the mirror could also be wishing or hoping for the superhuman ability to disappear from the limelight when the pressures mount.

Allowing the viewer into the privacy of one of the most vulnerable and intimate moments of Kendrick's career is a bold and powerful mode of expression for the rapper and the aggressiveness with which Kendrick raps the lyrics show that, as was the motivation for the positive and uplifting antithesis track "i", Kendrick is

---

[36] Dorian Lynskey, "Kendrick Lamar: 'I am Trayvon Martin. I'm all of these kids'," *The Guardian.* June 21, 2015.

"attacking" his depression. He says, "if you don't attack it, it will attack you. If you sit around moping, feeling sad and stagnant, it's gonna eat you alive. I had to make that record. It's a reminder. It makes me feel good."[37] By addressing these emotions artistically head-on, Kendrick is using agency and taking control of his internal battle. On the track his conscience tells him "I know your secrets nigga/mood swings is frequent nigga", again threatening to expose him to the cultural scene in hip hop where depression and mental illness are considered taboo.

Although "u" is the crucial track in which Kendrick admits and battles with his mental illness, depression continues to rear its ugly head throughout *To Pimp a Butterfly*. At the end of the track "Hood Politics", Kendrick recites the central poem that keeps building throughout the album and recalls, "but that didn't stop survivors guilt/going back and forth/trying to convince myself the stripes I earned/or maybe how A-1 my foundation was/but while my loved ones was fighting/a continuous war back in the city/I was entering a new one". Again, Kendrick connects his mental state with the guilt he feels for not being home and helping his community with the problems they face. Kendrick's internal battle with depression is intimately connected with his responsibility to his city and his people who are battling racial inequality and systematic racism. Kendrick has escaped the hood, something that many rappers dream of, but the hood has a grasp on Kendrick that he can't escape, eventually leading him back "home" later in the album.

Kendrick's multi-ego continues to appear in "The Blacker the Berry" as he mentions being schizophrenic, which seems a more complicated and accurate representation of W.E.B. DuBois's concept of double-consciousness. Instead of being mentally ill, Kendrick is using his multi-ego'd schizophrenia as a source of artistic power and expression. With the dichotomy of the negativity of "u" and the positive uplift of "i", Kendrick shows that his emotions (like everyone's) are varied and ever-changing. In "i" he raps, "in front of a dirty double-

---

[37] Josh Ellis, "The Trials of Kendrick Lamar," Rolling Stone, June 22, 2015.

mirror they found me" which is a throwback reference to the mirror he raps about in "u" and the mirror he is looking at in the "God is Gangsta" video. The "dirty double-mirror" has multiple connotations as it represents both his mental state but also alludes to a police interrogation. In Kendrick's world, the police are as "dirty" as his own conscience, both being agitators of his mental illness. With "i" Kendrick begins to find self-love but, as we see in the track's music video, he is still reminded of his lowest point in the hotel room when he contemplated suicide, as the camera pans passed the window of a man with a gun to his head. Kendrick—embodying all the different personas that make up his multi-ego—has been there and is no longer afraid to face whichever part of his multi-ego shows up in the mirror.

Time Travel Identity Exploration

The most effective way in which Kendrick muses upon his mental state and his depression is by time traveling through space and time to reflect on formative moments and people that eventually lead him to the realization of self-love. These moments are not limited to the life Kendrick has literally lived but can be representations of past lives or formative moments in African-American history which shape the Kendrick's present world. This internal reflection is combative to the negative internalization of depression that Kendrick battles and allows him to understand the how and why of where he has come from, where his life is currently and where he will go in the future both personally and with his artistic career. The past, present, and future are imperative and cyclical in the Afrofuturist aesthetic, constantly supporting, enlightening, and manipulating the understanding of each conception of time, and the best way to examine the different elements of time is to boundlessly travel through them and reflect.

Kendrick time travels throughout *To Pimp a Butterfly* beginning in the first verse of the first track "Wesley's Theory" as he takes on the persona of himself as a young artist to set up his personal evolution. Kendrick, like many young rappers, depicts his younger self as focused on money, women, guns, and material wealth. These short-sighted obsessions are undoubtedly what Kendrick finds frustrating about the current state of the rap industry, which he consistently compares to slavery, as if he sees up-and-coming rappers as slaves to the game, whether that be to the record companies or to the quest for material wealth.

In "King Kunta", Kendrick alludes to this connection by taking on the role of both King and slave, representing the highest and lowest levels of society while asserting that he is the King of hip hop. Even if he is at the top of the game, he is still a slave within the system, whether that system is the music industry or America in general, because the system is rigged against African-American men like him. That is not to say that being the King of hip hop doesn't hold a very important place within the industry and society. Kendrick is proud of his success but also is grounded in knowing that, with power comes responsibility and as ruler he must lead and not sit ideally by atop his throne. Kunta Kinte, the rebellious slave from the Alex Haley novel and subsequent movie "Roots: The Saga of an American Family" is Kendrick's way of identifying with the insubordinate character and proclaim, along with being the King of hip hop, that he is also here to challenge the status quo. He raps that everyone wants to "cut the legs off" of King Kunta because he is running the game as King. "Everyone" is representative of other rappers who want to challenge his claim to the throne but also people that are uncomfortable seeing a wealthy black man succeed in America. He references both Richard Pryor's drug use and Bill Clinton's infidelity on the track to juxtapose how a wealthy and influential black man can be brought down by addiction just as the most powerful man in the world can. Kendrick is cognizant of the pitfalls before him as King and knows that both external and internal forces will try to knock him from his throne. In the first excerpt of the album's poem Kendrick recites, "I remember you was conflicted, misusing your influence" and "King Kunta" explores the idea of Kendrick as an influencer, and how he has grown from "a peasant, to a prince, to a motherfucking king".

The misuse of his influence as the King of hip hop is displayed in the next track "These Walls" where Kendrick travels back to a likely fictionalized house party in which he attempts to have sex with a woman whose man is in jail for killing one of Kendrick's friends. "These Walls" represent the walls of a woman's vagina, the walls of Kendrick's mind and consciousness, the walls of racial oppression, the defensive walls that people put up in both relationships with other people and their own psyche, and the walls of the prison cell that the man, who Kendrick seeks revenge from, is trapped in. Kendrick uses his fame and power to have sex with the woman but instead of reveling in the success of his revenge, his conscience gets the better of him and he feels guilty for abusing his power which, as we know, will eventually exacerbate his internal struggle with depression. Just as he is unable to escape being institutionalized in the previous track, Kendrick relates how he is unable to escape his consciousness, the situation he finds himself in at the house party, or his temptation. As he plans to seduce the woman, Kendrick raps, "I can feel your reign when it cries/gold lives inside you". The play on the word rain/reign throws back to Kendrick as King and the depressive residual effects of rain, as the woman cries for her man and the idea of cheating on him, but also the raining wetness of her vagina and the cries of passion as she has sex with Kendrick. Kendrick, as King, seeks the gold inside her which equates to revenge against his foe. He continues, "these walls are vulnerable, exclamation/interior pink, color coordinated/I interrogated, every nook and cranny" as he continues with the intimate connection between the woman's vagina and his own brain/consciousness. Both are pink, vulnerable, and color coordinated as he examines both the woman's vagina and his own consciousness vigorously.

In the third verse of "These Walls", Kendrick travels from the house party directly to the man in prison whose woman he seduced. Kendrick expresses resentment in his voice, possibly both for the man killing his friend and because Kendrick's plot of revenge was unsuccessful and backfired by intensifying his depression. Kendrick tells the man, "it's too late/your destiny accepted your fate" but whose fate is Kendrick really talking about as he raps, "so when you play this song, rewind the first verse/about me abusing my power so you can hurt/about me and her in the shower whenever she horny/about me and her in the afterhours of the morning/about her baby daddy currently serving life"? Although the verse seemingly portrays Kendrick telling the man in prison that he had sex with his woman, Kendrick is also reminding himself that he has abused his power. By stating in the last line "about her baby daddy" it is revealed that Kendrick is in fact talking to himself and not in the prison cell with the man, and that he must be reminded of the vengeful act every time he hears this song.

There are many other instances throughout the album where Kendrick either transforms himself into another being, time, or place, playing with the concepts of space and time to tell the story of his past, present, and future world. In the third verse of "Momma", Kendrick takes on the role of a little boy he meets in Africa (possibly a version of himself from another life) that is trying to teach him about his heritage and ancestry. In "You Ain't Gotta Lie (Momma Said)", Kendrick voices his own mother, advising him to be humble and return to Compton to help his community. Now that Kendrick has returned home in "Hood Politics", he travels back in time and raps in a higher voice to represent his younger self, when the hood was all he knew, to discuss American politics in the second verse and the rap industry in the third verse. Even guest singer Bilal in "Institutionalized" sings the hook in a nasally voice to represent Kendrick's deceased Grandma as she speaks to him from the afterlife. By assuming the identities of these various characters, Kendrick time travels to speak to himself in present, and allowing himself to escape his internalized struggle with depression to give an outside perspective into his own life and career.

In an interview for GQ Magazine with legendary producer Rick Rubin, Kendrick was asked where he gets a lot of his inspiration for writing. Kendrick responded by saying the following:

> Man, it's mainly kids. Man, I always say this. Kids bug me out because they have no fear in nothing. Like nothing. I sit there and I talk to kids. Like, my little niece is two years old but she fears nothing and

> has no concept of reality as we know it. That always inspired me to write for some reason man. It don't necessarily have to be whatever the actual child is pertaining to but talking to them gives me a moment to step back and look at the world for what I know it [...].[38]

Kendrick then refers to himself as "the biggest kid" and that child-like nature, or mental exercise of time travelling back to his childhood, allows Kendrick to separate himself from the reality he finds himself in, and write from a different perspective.

    Kendrick also imagines himself as a present day and futuristic superhero. Twice on the uplifting track "i", Kendrick says "fi-fie-fo-fum" likening himself to a giant big enough to optimistically trudge forth and not be stopped by negativity, his depression, or systematic racial oppression. Even comic superpower Marvel connected themes of *To Pimp a Butterfly* with the *Guardians of the Galaxy* world as they created a superhero version of the album art, invoking that the black disenfranchised people represented on the cover can be superhuman. During his performance of "i" on Saturday Night Live,[39] Kendrick appears with his hair wild and half-braided, with completely black eyes like an otherworldly alien as he connects the hood to outer space and the poor black man to the supernatural, powerful, and cool. As Billboard points out, Kendrick "teased further ambitions" with the performance as he "evoked Method Man" with the black contact lenses and Ol' Dirty Bastard with the "riot of braids"[40]. Kendrick said "I don't want people to take away how cute I look, or how the light is shining off my chain. I want you to take away a great-ass performance." It was

---

[38] "Watch What Happens When Kendrick Lamar Meets Rick Rubin for an Epic Interview," *GQ*, October 20, 2016.

[39] Alex Young, "Kendrick Lamar delivers an SNL performance for the ages-watch," *Consequence of* Sound, November 15, 2015.

[40] Gavin Edwards, "Billboard Cover: Kendrick Lamar on Ferguson, Leaving Iggy Azalea Alone and Why 'We're in the Last Days'," *Billboard*. January 9, 2015.

a powerful show, as Kendrick reached into the past to invoke artists who influenced him and to connect the streets where he grew up to his superhuman ability to rock a mic and give an otherworldly performance.

In an interview with Mass Appeal, Kendrick describes the superhero he imagines himself to be.[41] The hero's name is Hardbody and doesn't wear a uniform, "no mask no nothing" who projects straight love "in a world full of hate". Kendrick imagines Hardbody spreading love on the streets as it relates to gang violence and also in regard to discrimination. He believes the energy of love spreads like wildfire and by spreading love, Hardbody can realistically change the world. Hardbody's archenemy? Lucifer disguised as a woman. Lucy is seductive and deceitful and as we know, one of the main characters in Kendrick's *To Pimp a Butterfly*. Imagining oneself as superhuman or otherworldly is a common trope in Afrofuturist music and Eshun's concept of multi-ego, a source of power that artists can adopt to express their true or imagined selves and what they hope to accomplish with their art.

The External Pressures of Speaking for the People

Although many dark themes exist in *To Pimp a Butterfly*, it seems that the overarching message is one of positive transformation, both for Kendrick personally and for the African-American community as a whole. Kendrick's personal struggles with depression and ultimate quest for finding self-love (expressed in the metaphor of the transformation of a caterpillar to a butterfly) can also be applied to the struggles the African-American community faces in America's current cultural landscape which is discussed later in this project. As a role model, Kendrick has the power to speak not only *to* the people, but at times *for* the people, in expressing their frustrations with the current political and social climate of racism in America and their hopes and

---

[41] MP, "Super... With Kendrick Lamar," *Mass Appeal*. May 1, 2015.

dreams for their future inclusion and universal acceptance into society. Make no mistake about it, and with adopting the Afrofuturist metaphor of African-Americans being the first alien abductees, African-Americans are still treated as aliens in what is just as much their home as it is anyone else's. Underlying (and overt) racism is prevalent in modern culture[42] and it is a wonder to think what it will take for the nation to evolve towards an era of post-racism.

      Kendrick begins the album with the message of self-love and cultural uplift by sampling Jamaican singer Boris Gardiner's "Every Nigga is a Star" from the film of the same name. The purpose of the song was to change the perception of the word "nigga" during the 1970s and encourage a connotation of racial pride within the black community. Just as previously discussed, one of the aims of Afrofuturist art is to take oppressive identifications of Otherness and make them sources of power. Outkast made it cool to be ATLiens just as "Every Nigga is a Star" attempted to take a racial slur and empower it. *To Pimp a Butterfly* highlights the metaphor of a caterpillar's transformation into a beautiful butterfly and attempts to transform some of the negative perceptions of the African-American community into those of strength and resilience.

      Kendrick continues to do this by tapping into his multi-ego, but instead of doing so to understand the different identifying elements of his own persona as argued in the previous section, he also explores the realms of his multi-ego to represent multiple characters within the African-American community and give voice to those seemingly voiceless factions of society. In "Institutionalized", Kendrick manipulates his voice more than ever, rapping high-pitched as he speaks from the mindset of someone still trapped in the oppressive structure of the hood and who is numb to the killing, death, drugs, money, and greed. In the second verse, Kendrick has a conversation with a friend that he takes to the BET Awards, playing the role of both characters and rapping back and forth. The friend is frustrated with the

---

[42] See 2016 election cycle and its aftermath, the opposition to the Black Lives Matter Movement, etc..

flamboyant waste of money that rappers show, especially during a recession, and plots to rob the rich people at the awards show. As a wealthy rapper, Kendrick is unable to directly address his own frustrations with the bling culture of hip hop, but instead gives voice to the common man who struggles to make ends meet while watching hip hop artists "make it rain" on strippers, drive cars and wear chains worth hundreds of thousands of dollars, and live unabashedly frivolous while other people scratch and claw to survive. This frustration is not exclusive to the African-American community or even the United States as we see the wage gap exponentially increase over time and poverty remain a major cultural problem across the globe.

The music video for "These Walls" is also an opportunity to Kendrick to represent the fans (or not) that are watching his career develop. The opening title for the video reads "Behind These Walls: A Black Comedy" suggesting the light-hearted video has a darker overarching message and that it stars black actors. The camera pans to three black men imprisoned. One man claims that Kendrick is the reason he is imprisoned, as he describes a party in a motel which serves as the setting for much of the video. This blame can be seen as a literal interpretation of the story in the song or the figurative guilt that Kendrick feels in becoming successful and escaping the struggles faced by young black men. The camera pans from room to room of the motel, following the walls, and showing scenes of black people having sex, gambling, and engaging in general party debauchery. Kendrick is shown up against a wall of a room, dancing with a bodacious woman (possibly the woman of the man who is in prison), as two other women are videotaping him, representing the eyes of the fans, media, and country as "these walls are talking". The force of the woman's body dancing against Kendrick causes him to break through the wall and fall backwards as he raps the end of the first verse. The camera pans out into the other rooms and hallways, showing aggressive behavior of black men and women wearing gangsta fashions. The video cuts to the inside of a car with three black men. Kendrick is riding shotgun while actor Terry Crews is yelling hysterically about how he is going to kill someone. Kendrick tells him to shut up and that they are simply going to rob the man. Cut to Terry Crews continuing to yell aggressively and looking for the man he is threatening to kill, when he is joined by Kendrick, they find themselves on the stage of a talent show where they begin a comical dancing performance that is like a mime black-on-black crime. This scene is a commentary on how America sits back watching and being entertained by black on black violence. The scene cuts back to the man in prison remembering the party. He shows up and, seeing Kendrick with his woman, the man doesn't get angry because he "has respect for" Kendrick, probably because of his fame. The man joins Kendrick in receiving lap dances from a slew of women before the police arrive and arrest him for apparently rear ending a police car. Finally, Kendrick is seen ominously rapping the third verse to the man in prison while his girl has sex with another man. The inmate in prison makes a hole in the "wall" of his cell and looks in to what is assumed to be the sex scene. Despite the tragic nature of the story, the video and song have a light-hearted feel, depicting the complicated emotions Kendrick feels about his fame and the power that comes with it. In telling the story in the song, Kendrick can examine and evaluate the different perspectives of not only the plot that evolves, but of the complicated thematic implications of racial tensions within the race, between black men and the police, the judicial system and being incarcerated, between black men and black women, and the hypocrisy of how America treats the people that are trapped within the walls of an oppressive system.

    The struggle between Kendrick's position as role model/spokesperson and how he feels people view him is constant. In the intro to "Hood Politics" we hear a voicemail on Kendrick's phone where his friend worries he has changed and gotten into "weirdo rap shit" because he is now "gospel rappin'".[43] Part of the politics of the hood is that Kendrick must find a balance between staying true to himself, his mission, and the black community, while also trying to stay hood and gangsta. On the track he insures that he has found that balance and is still hood as he raps, "I been A-1[44] since day one, you

---

[43] Similar to Andre 3000 on OutKast's "Return of the 'G'".

nigga boo boo[45]". The first verse finds Kendrick deviating from the political narrative of the previous songs to straight spit (rap), reminding the listeners that he still knows where he comes from as he says, "I don't give a fuck about no politics in rap, my nigga" (which we know is not true). Kendrick is letting the other side of his ego out, the side that was raised and influenced by Compton.

Kendrick revels in the role of spokesperson for his people and generation as he raps in "Momma", "I can be your advocate/I can preach for you if you tell me what the matter is". He says this to a little boy he meets in Africa (potentially a young version of himself) but also to all his fans and to anyone that needs a powerful black man as an advocate. In the final track "Mortal Man", Kendrick realizes he is the new voice of the people as he channels Malcolm X, Martin Luther King Jr., Nelson Mandela, and Tupac Shakur, all extremely influential and sometimes controversial figures in American history. These figures were all outspoken in their wish to change the world for the better, especially for African-Americans. Kendrick worries that his time on this earth is limited and that he needs to make an impact on his people before his time is up. On Nelson Mandela's influence on him, he raps, "the ghost of Mandela, hope my flows they propel it/let these words be your earth and moon/you consume every message/as I lead this army make room for mistakes and depression/and with that being said my nigga, let me ask this question". After his trip to South Africa, Kendrick wishes to carry the torch of Nelson Mandela, but he also recognizes he will still make mistakes and wonders if his fans will stick by him no matter what. Kendrick admires Mandela for not seeking revenge against those who imprisoned him but instead focusing on bringing blacks and whites together, a goal that Kendrick wishes to adopt as he hopes to lead by example for the next generation. On the track, he also references Moses, Huey Newton, JFK, Jackie Robinson, Jesse Jackson, and Michael Jackson who all, in their own way, had major impacts on the past, present, and future of oppressed people of color. Kendrick

---

[44] Meaning excellent.
[45] Meaning excrement.

clearly wishes to be that influential leader and spokesperson who changes the trajectory of the future for African Americans.

The external pressures to become an advocate and spokesperson for the African-American community are propelled by an internal guidance he finds through religion. One thing that religion and Afrofuturism have in common is that both pull from the history and traditions of the past to envision a brighter future for its people. Kendrick, an admittedly spiritual and religious person, takes on multiple religious roles in *To Pimp a Butterfly* including preacher, advocate, and eternal nemesis of Lucy aka Lucifer. Many people including The New York Times have dubbed him the "Hip Hop Messiah"[46] and instead of shying away from the extraordinary honor and responsibility that comes along with that title, Kendrick embraces it wholeheartedly. In an interview with XXL magazine Kendrick discussed this responsibility:

> When I try to soak it all in, that's the only thing that kind've scare me, feel me? Life is sad in general and I'm meeting these different people every day. It kind've snaps me back into reality outside of what I do. Outside of the girls, outside of the cars, the money, it really ain't that important when you meeting somebody that's still in the struggle. These the people that live their lives in dark spaces, every day, you know, and they use my music as some sort of tool to keep going, almost like a Bible, you know? These kids feel like they got nothing to believe in but they see me and say, "Kendrick, I believe in you. I believe in your music." And what happens it puts me in some type of space where it's almost like some type of worship or responsibility, but I know it. I can see it.[47]

---

[46] Joe Coscarelli, "Kendrick Lamar on His New Album and the Weight of Clarity," *The New York Times*, March 16, 2015.

[47] "Writer At War: Kendrick Lamar's XXL Cover Story," *XXL*, January 6, 2015.

Lucy, the main antagonist throughout *To Pimp a Butterfly* represents multiple obstacles and temptations that Kendrick is up against. "She" represents the devil as understood in Christianity that Kendrick must internally grapple with as he progresses in his life and his career, but Lucy also represents external elements working against Kendrick and his people. Elements such as a music industry which Kendrick feels, as discussed earlier, treats its black artists like slaves, and America, a country which has failed and continues to fail the African-American community with subjected and systematic racism in the form of wealth inequality, the mass incarceration of young black men, police brutality, under representation of elected officials, and a culture of racism (particularly) in the South as a residual effect of the slave days. How Kendrick addresses religion on *To Pimp a Butterfly* will be discussed in a later chapter (6), but first we must grab a front row seat to his otherworldly battle with his nemesis Lucy.

Kendrick vs. Lucy/Lucifer/America/Music Industry

No tale of self-discovery, reflection, and triumph over the odds is complete without the ominous threat of a seemingly unbeatable foe. Kendrick Lamar's antagonist in his personal fight for depression and his quest for the hip hop throne is an amalgamation of both the systematic and spiritual powers against not only him, but other rappers trying to make it in the industry and African-American's trying to find equality in America. *To Pimp a Butterfly*'s "Lucy" takes on many forms, disguising herself in a variety of ways to manipulate and trick Kendrick and those that he speaks for. A common trope throughout the history of storytelling, Kendrick must prevail and avenge history to insure a prosperous future for his people.

In the first track "Wesley's Theory", Lucy takes the form of Uncle Sam, tempting him, as a rich black rapper, into sabotaging himself by living an outlandish lifestyle and spending all his money to bolster and sustain the American capitalist system that thrives on the debt of its people and perpetuates the systematic oppression of the poor and disenfranchised. The title "Wesley's Theory" alludes to movie star Wesley Snipes' tax problems and hinting at the warning that no matter how successful you may be at one point, especially if you are black, there is always a chance in America that the capitalist system or the government will propagate a fall from your social position. The track sets the stage for the temptation that Kendrick faces to fall into the trap of the rap industry, lose himself in money and fame, and relinquish his place on top of the music world.

Kendrick battles "Lucy" in the best way he knows how, by adopting the role of a preacher. In "u" he raps in an almost manic tone, preaching to both himself and his audience. Preachers are messengers but to find a congregation, it is most effective to join the audience in sharing their pain and own struggles. After Kendrick's second album *good kid, m.A.A.d. city*, Kendrick was baptized giving him legitimacy in the role he takes on as preacher. In an interview with The New York Times reviewer Joe Coscarelli, Kendrick said, "I know every artist feels this way, but in order for it to come across on record for your average 9-to-5-er is the tricky part. I have to make it where you truly understand: This is me pouring out my soul on the record. You're gonna feel it because you too have pain. It might not be like mine, but you're gonna feel it."[48] In order to preach to and for his people, Kendrick must first be able to identify with their own personal struggles and make them his own. The responsibility of battling the devil is great, and Kendrick bears it throughout *To Pimp a Butterfly*.

In "Alright", we see Kendrick's voice shift in the first verse as he plays Lucy attempting to corrupt him and take his soul. In "For Sale? (Interlude)", Kendrick again plays Lucy and talks to Kendrick as if they are intimately connected lovers, like he has sold his soul to the Devil. In "Momma", the outro finds Kendrick back in conversation with Lucy as he frantically repeats "jump, jump, jump". The jump is both meant as a leap into the quest for greater knowledge about himself and his people, but also hints at his relationship with Lucy and how his

---

[48] Joe Coscarelli, "Kendrick Lamar on His New Album and the Weight of Clarity," *The New York Times*, March 16, 2015.

sins sometimes make him want to commit suicide. This play on the word "jump" co-mingles Kendrick's internal panic and depression with his journey of finding self-love. His relationship with the temptation of the Devil, his frustrations with America, and his distrust with the music industry are complicated, and he addresses them by exploring his multi-ego and having intimate conversations and confrontations with "Lucy" who represents them all.

Ultimately, Kendrick's multi-egos allow him to successfully address what is going on in his world; positively, negatively, internally, and externally. With the help of so many other talented musicians, who all possess their own community of multi-egos, Kendrick is able to create a universal and comprehensive album that follows his own personal journey. Of the recording of the album, Terrace Martin suggests that *To Pimp a Butterfly* follows the model of old jazz albums from Afrofuturist artists Miles Davis and John Coltrane: "It's kind of like the Miles Davis concept too, where his whole album is full of leaders. But, leaders that follow him—[TPAB] is a fine demonstration of having the biggest ego in the room be the music."[49] The music (and Kendrick) ultimately prevail as Kendrick raps in the self-love anthem "i", "I went to war last night (Night, night, night, night, night)/I've been dealing with depression ever since an adolescent/duckin' every other blessin', I can never see the message/I could never take the lead; I could never bob and weave/from a negative and letting them annihilate me/and it's evident I'm moving at a meteor speed".

---

[49] Natalie Weiner, "How Kendrick Lamar Transformed Into 'The John Coltrane of Hip-Hop' on 'To Pimp a Butterfly," *Billboard*, March 26, 2015.

4.

Moving at a Meteor Speed: Time Travelling through the History of Afrofuturist Music

Music is all connected — we put different labels on it but hip-hop, in a way, already is jazz. Like funk is jazz and jazz is funk, jazz is hip-hop. It's all the same thing. If you really can hear it, it doesn't matter if you have a message behind it — you'll understand. Especially American music, especially African-American music — it's really one thing.

– Kamasi Washington[50]

Kendrick Lamar is undoubtedly a hip hop artist, but anyone that listens to *To Pimp a Butterfly* understands that it is no ordinary hip hop album. Blending elements of jazz, funk, and electronic music, Kendrick and the various producers of the album reach back into the annuls of African-American and Afrofururist music to create a soundscape representative of the past, present, and future of black music. Just as Kendrick time travels throughout the album to the slave days and to visit his younger self, he also time travels through his influences and those who came before him and blazed a futuristic trail of musical aesthetics.

With the first track "Wesley's Theory", the album constructs the pillars of the four major Afrofuturist genres of past and present as guest George Clinton brings the funk, virtuoso Thundercat supplies the jazz fusion bass lines, producer Flying Lotus provides the technological electronic future, and Dr. Dre roots us in hip hop culture. As Clinton says on the track, "when the four corners of the cocoon collide [...]" the metaphor of Kendrick's transformation from caterpillar to butterfly

---

[50] Natalie Weiner, "How Kendrick Lamar Transformed Into 'The John Coltrane of Hip-Hop' on 'To Pimp a Butterfly," *Billboard*, March 26, 2015.

runs parallel to his bringing together of the four corners/pillars of Afrofuturist music from which he has evolved. Dr. Dre (one of Kendrick's most important mentors) makes his only appearance on the record to remind Kendrick of the pitfalls of fame in hip hop. Clinton also speaks to Kendrick's success and popularity and how far Kendrick will fall if he loses his way or fails, warning him to "look both ways before you cross my mind", a caution to Kendrick of the rabbit hole that is self-exploration, self-discovery, and personal evolution. Clinton and Dr. Dre embody the opulent past while Flying Lotus and Thundercat represent the promising future of Afrofuturism. Each one of these genres and artists, and how they relate to the Afrofuturist aesthetic, will be examined in this chapter.

Future from the Past: George Clinton

In the middle of the night, just hours after Kendrick Lamar prematurely released *To Pimp a Butterfly*, Afrofuturist electronic producer Flying Lotus took to social media and began tweeting about his involvement on what he called, the "classic" album. Of the opening track "Wesley's Theory", which Fly Lo produced, he tweeted, "When I played [Kendrick] that beat he asked me who I imagined on it. I laughed and said [George Clinton]. I never thought it would actually happen" but in Kendrick and Clinton's limitless world of Afrofuturist possibilities, anything is imaginable.

1970s America found African-Americans in an unprecedented social situation. After the near 20-year political and philosophical battle of the Civil Rights Movement, the African-American community had long been ready to embrace their legally appropriated equality. As a systematically oppressed group, African-Americans could now imagine an American environment in which political, communal, and artistic expression could be even more effective in creating social consciousness and mobility. Although Sun Ra had previously introduced Afrofuturist themes in music as early as the 1950s, the post-civil rights stage was set for a larger audience, and an Afrofuturist movement which would change black identity and black music forever. Enter in Parliament-Funkadelic (or P-Funk); a music collective that's imagery and sound took Sun Ra's Afrofuturist vision to the masses and introduced a creative vehicle and cultural philosophy which led African-Americans into an equal rights era. As Afrofuturist author Ytasha Womack describes, "Afrofuturist music embodies the times while literally sounding out of this world"[51] and the George Clinton-led P-Funk embodied Afrofuturism. George Clinton's Parliament-Funkadelic assisted the African-American community in envisioning a post-civil rights America in which the future is present and oppressive limitations on the black individual are lifted, setting an example of communal involvement and social movement through futuristic artistic expression.

African-American expression through music is rooted in slavery, as individuals were forced to make the most of what they had access to in order to create music and, in the instance of slavery, they had little or nothing to work with technologically. Using their singing voices and making whatever percussive sounds they could manage, slaves held onto African heritage and culture through music regardless of slave-owners attempt to eliminate their history. In fact, nearly all aspects of black music are rooted in West African music traditions that were taken to America during the slave trade. Professor Reynaldo Anderson explains Afrofuturist representations of post-human identity by stating, "we're among the first alien abductees, kidnapped by strange people who take us over by ships and conduct scientific experiments on us. They bred us. They came up with a taxonomy of the people they bred: mulatto, octoroon, quadroon."[52] African-Americans have roots based in Otherness that resemble alien identity, and instead of shying away from this distinction, Afrofuturist artists adopt and adapt post-human identity as a powerful expression of self. Marlo David writes that, "[…] the idea of the post-human has been posited as a remedy by those within and outside of black cultural

---

[51] Ytasha L. Womack, Afrofuturism: The World of Black Sci-Fi and Fantasy Culture (Chicago: Lawrence Hill Books, 2013) 55.
[52] Ytasha L. Womack, Afrofuturism: The World of Black Sci-Fi and Fantasy Culture (Chicago: Lawrence Hill Books, 2013) 35.

studies, particularly in the space of futurist studies. As some would have it, in a post-human universe governed by zeroes and ones, the body ceases to matter, thereby fracturing and finally dissolving ties to racialized subjectivity, positionality, and 'self'."[53] The ideological binaries of race are blurred by post-humanizing an individual while archaic and arbitrary lines of difference are presumably considered taboo within a future of post-Otherness.

With P-Funk, George Clinton created an atmosphere inspired by post-human identity and outer space themes, allowing the American-American community to envision a futuristic environment they had previously been left out of. In his comprehensive account of the genre, *Funk*, Rickey Vincent writes of P-Funk, "their grandiose concepts, which preached redemptive powers of funk, their vast informal enterprise, and their powerful affirmation of common black folks, created a small-scale movement and large-scale following [...]"[54]. The message that P-Funk preached was different from the messages of Martin Luther King Jr. and other leaders of the Civil Right Movement era. Instead of preaching about the present or the relevant near future of the African-American community, P-Funk seemed to consider the future as now and preach about the possibilities of a distant future in which black America wasn't only equal, but the focal point of American identity. The mode in which P-Funk delivered its message was also a result of the effectiveness of the Civil Rights Movement's non-violent strategy. Vincent explains that P-Funk operated, "without polemics, militarism, or racially charged code words, Clinton's P-Funk placed the African American sensibility at the center of the universe, and ultimately at the center of *history*."[55] By continuing in the mode of civil rights leaders, P-Funk created an inclusive, fun, and light-hearted atmosphere of placing African-American identity at a place of extreme importance and cultural significance within the nation as a whole.

---

[53] Marlo David, "Afrofuturism and Post-Soul Possibility in Black Popular Music," *African American Review* 41.4, 2007. 695.
[54] Rickey Vincent, Funk: The Music, The People, and The Rhythm of The One (New York: St. Martin's Press, 1996) 231.
[55] Ibid, 254.

An important part of P-Funk's success was a result of their inclusive identity, offering black America an entertaining and complex communal identity that any individual could find appealing. By creating an artistic atmosphere of multiple bands, where individual musicians could freely move back and forth between projects at their will, Clinton introduced a new way of creating music where a community was encouraged, and competition was non-existent. Vincent argues that P-Funk, "playing as two bands, Funkadelic (playing 'rock,' which is associated with whites) and Parliament (soul for black radio), the notion of 'double consciousness' introduced by W.E.B. Du Bois in 1903 was exposed."[56] Although utilizing Du Bois' double consciousness notion is useful in describing the cross-racial likability of P-Funk's music, it falls short of describing the complexity of the group's multiple identities. To properly describe P-Funk's (and Clinton individually) multiplicity, we again call on Eshun's description of multi-egos discussed in chapter 3. Not only does Clinton take on the multi-egos of Dr. Funkenstein, the Prime Minister of Funk, bandleader, singer, songwriter, etc. but P-Funk also adopts multi-egos in the form or Parliament, Funkadelic, Bootsy's Rubber Band and other side projects stemming from the group. By working together as an artistic collective, P-Funk sets an example for the African-American community to work together towards social and political advancement. Vincent explains how this band who "appeared like a group of ghetto circus clowns […]"[57] transcended prior oppressive and systematic ideals of black America in the following passage.

> What appeared as two acts was actually one entity with many dimensions, as most African-Americans inevitably experience as a result of their struggle in a white country. Du Bois's reference to 'two warring ideals in one dark body' has dogged the racial experience in America, as racial minorities are

---

[56] Ibid, 235.
[57] Rickey Vincent, Funk: The Music, The People, and The Rhythm of The One (New York: St. Martin's Press, 1996) 234.

> constantly labeled as 'sellouts' when status,
> education, or success is realized. Yet P-Funk
> transcended this conundrum, as the notions of
> intellect, education, or sophistication were totally
> removed from any association with white status.
> Thus, P-Funk became the *ultimate* in African-
> American liberation.[58]

By describing P-Funk's image as that of circus clowns, Vincent simultaneously emphasizes the individuality of the different musicians through their own identity while alluding to the communal synchronization of circus performers. The members of P-Funk are in fact entertainers but moreover they serve as members of a liberating collective that undermines destructive stereotypes and limiting labels established and upheld by the white normative status quo. After the Civil Rights Movement was an opportune time to dissemble negative aspects of black identity and re-create the African-American community focusing on positive collectivity, just as 2015 was an opportune time for *To Pimp a Butterfly* to address the current socio-racial landscape in American and for "Alright" to become the anthem for the Black Lives Matter movement.

It is important to remember that the Afrofuturist aesthetic does not only look to the future, but also re-imagines and honors the past of black experience through art. As Womack writes, "what connects these cultural productions are futuristic counternarratives that speak to the intersections of history and progress, tradition and innovation, technology and memory, the authentic and engineered, analog and digital within spaces of African diasporic culture."[59] This connection between past, present and future is what makes P-Funk a perfect example of what an Afrofuturist band can be. The collective group of musicians represent a history of African and African-American culture, while looking to the future and imagining the potential of an

---

[58] Ibid, 235.
[59] Marlo David, "Afrofuturism and Post-Soul Possibility in Black Popular Music," African American Review 41.4, 2007. 698.

unencumbered, free, and liberated African-American community. For Vincent, "P-Funk was and is more than a music style; it is a philosophy of life that for some approaches a religious creed."[60] The bands transcend entertainment, entering a realm of spiritual enlightenment and awakening. Here, Vincent highlights P-Funk's connection to the roots of African-American religion, while also emphasizing P-Funk's innovative philosophizing into the future. Vincent continues: "The music and concepts drew listeners into a coded philosophy of black nationhood, of freedom of expression and personal salvation though the use of symbols and double meanings that had deep roots in black music and religious traditions."[61] P-Funk includes this ode to the past and look to the future in their 1975 album *Mothership Connection*. The song "Mothership Connection (Star Child)" incorporates lyrics which call back to "well-known themes in black religion"[62] as the chorus chants "swing down, sweet chariot/stop and let me ride".[63] Here, Parliament and Clinton pay homage to black belief systems and religion, while simultaneously asking the "chariot" or "mothership" to stop and let them ride into the future on a new vehicle; one that is a spaceship which allows for a new re-examination of traditional African-American beliefs.

The imagination of Clinton is a key component of P-Funk's Afrofuturist agenda. In an Afrofuturist band, the imaginative limits are the limits of the universe and the futuristic imagination. With P-Funk, Clinton imagines a mythology, centered on a "Mothership" which serves as the catalyst for the introduction of "The Funk" and the liberating and unifying message that P-Funk brings. The idea came to Clinton and bassist Bootsy Collins on night as, "we saw this light bouncing from one side of the street to the other. It happened a few times and I [Clinton] made a comment that 'the Mothership was angry with us for giving up the funk without permission.' Just then the light hit the car. All the street lights went out, and there weren't any cars

---

[60] Rickey Vincent, Funk: The Music, The People, and The Rhythm of The One (New York: St. Martin's Press, 1996) 253.
[61] Ibid, 254.
[62] Ibid, 254.
[63] Parliament, *Mothership Connection*, (Casablanca: 1975).

around [...]."[64] The mothership image became a central thematic image for the group, allowing for an other-worldly, outer-space, and futuristic aesthetic that seemingly touched every one of the band's creative decisions. The lyrics on the band's *Mothership Connection* LP evoke a simultaneously futuristic and Afrocentric message as P-Funk sings about taking the mothership to "return to claim the pyramids".[65] This reclamation of heritage is important as the band uses imaginative and futuristic modes to declare pride in an historic accomplishment like building the pyramids. P-Funk seemed to be saying, until now, black America has not had the opportunity or the means to be as prideful as they rightfully should be, but now in a post-Civil Rights Movement America, the time has come for Afrocentric and futuristic pride. Vincent explains this hybridity of past/future and Afrocentric/Eurocentric by stating, "[...] P-Funk confiscated European musical aesthetics as a way of symbolizing just how much of Western civilization had been internalized by African-Americans, while the streetwise sensibilities of P-Funk continues to affirm the untenable bond on black/African consciousness within the group."[66] Not only does P-Funk's musical aesthetic symbolize an Afrocentric/Eurocentric hybridity representative of African-American culture, but their Afrofuturist aesthetic introduced black culture into a world of science fiction previously exclusive of white America. Seemingly in response to white science fiction writer's complete dismissal of inclusion of African-Americas as any significant part of their imagined future, "P-Funk's fantastic science fiction created a series of spectacular 'otherworlds' that Africans could inhabit freely, in which one could be loving, caring, sensual, psychedelic, and nasty without fear of cosmic retribution, and whites simply did not exist."[67] Without being overly anti-inclusionary, P-Funk was able to create a sense of African-American futuristic imagination, that simultaneously showed the science fiction community

---

[64] Rickey Vincent, Funk: The Music, The People, and The Rhythm of The One (New York: St. Martin's Press, 1996) 240.
[65] Parliament, Mothership Connection, (Casablanca: 1975).
[66] Rickey Vincent, Funk: The Music, The People, and The Rhythm of The One (New York: St. Martin's Press, 1996) 235.
[67] Ibid, 244.

that the future is a place where black people belong while bringing together to entertain a large audience that was interested in the future and the funk.

The religiosity of P-Funk as a group, not only brought together a large community of followers of the band, but also contained a message of individual responsibility and liberation. Mirroring the multiple and changing members of the bands, that contributed and shared freely as individual musicians, P-Funk sent messages of communal cooperation and personal agency which worked in concoction with the newly acquired civil rights of African-Americans. A message of unity within the community and a personal responsibility of what to do with new found rights, spoke to many followers who saw P-Funk's message as an example of spiritual guidance. Vincent explains how this is based in African spirituality in writing, "the African spiritual root of The Funk is important because the essence of funk music, as well as the *funk attitude*, is a return to certain traditional ways, among which are the basics of music-making; a celebration of the earthly, funky, emotionally vital way of life; and a cosmology of 'oneness' in which everything and everyone in the universe is interconnected."[68] The "oneness" that is created is the Civil Rights Movement as a whole which served as an example of what macro-cooperation and communal effort can accomplish. Oneness and interconnectivity are futuristic concepts while also being based in Afrocentric spirituality. However, American freedom as well as the freedom granted to African-Americans after the Civil Rights Movement call for individual freedoms as well, and a looking within oneself in self-reflection of what it means to be not only an African-American, but a human citizen of the world. Vincent explains this self-reflection and George Clinton's aim at empowering the individual by arguing that, "around the world, religious systems that are based on spiritual cultivation give power to the *individual* to attain higher realms. Clinton's funk attempts this. It is designed to empower the listener to

---

[68] Rickey Vincent, Funk: The Music, The People, and The Rhythm of The One (New York: St. Martin's Press, 1996) 258.

obtain self-knowledge, rather than follow a certain lead, and the more graphic the knowledge, the more self-aware the individual."[69] This futuristic empowerment that Clinton strives for comes on the heels of a social and cultural empowerment resulting from civil rights victories of the 1950s and 1960s. Clinton and P-Funk attempted to take the unprecedented empowerment of black American into the next era of African-American history as the group's music and futuristic aesthetic gained wide popularity and a passionate following.

P-Funk's Afrofuturist thematics spanned the breadth of their creative output. The group did not simply limit the futurist themes to lyrics and costumes but created an entire science fiction back story to accompany the music. Along with promoting communal involvement and independent responsibility, P-Funk wished to change the way African-Americans were portrayed in the media and entertainment world, by promoting positive depictions of blackness and to give encouraging examples in contrast with status quo portrayals of black America in the 1970s. Vincent relates P-Funk's intentions as combating, "the relentless barrage of negative information about black people portrayed in the media, the absence of visible black advocates in the public eye, and the very semantic foundation of the language that associated white with 'good' and black with 'bad' can be overwhelming to a black child. P-Funk began to turn these notions on their heads."[70] P-Funk again wished to take black America into a future which is starkly different from the past oppression African-Americans were historically subjugated to. This was especially important for young African-Americans who would now grow up in an America where their Otherness could be viewed as a source of empowerment.

The creation of funk as a musical genre, and specifically George Clinton's artistic avenues through the bands Parliament and Funkadelic, allowed for a continuation of Afrofuturist representations in music in the 70s, 80s and beyond. Clinton, who was inspired by both

---

[69] Ibid, 260.
[70] Rickey Vincent, Funk: The Music, The People, and The Rhythm of The One (New York: St. Martin's Press, 1996) 257.

Sun Ra and Jimi Hendrix, created another sonic fiction to tell a back story of himself and his bands in which the members served as transporters of Funk music from outer space to Earth. Clinton adopted his own persona of otherworldly colorful hair and flamboyant fashion while implementing alien-inspired album art and a futuristic live show. P-Funk's performances included a "mothership" that was said to have carried the band from outer space to the stage. Womack argues that Sun Ra and Clinton are the two fathers of Afrofuturist music as she writes, "the idea of a song mythology from the cosmos, high-flying African-inspired space costumes, wordplay that challenged logic, and the use of traditional and electronic instruments to redefine sounds and push for universal love were established by Sun Ra and George Clinton."[71] Not only did Clinton expand and introduce the genre of Funk to a large audience through electronic technology and instrumentation, but he assumed the alien identity of post-slavery African-Americans to explore the future of black identity in America. The live shows alluded to a futuristic world of endless possibility and as Clinton describes, "'I had to find another place where they hadn't perceived black people to be and that was on a spaceship'" and the image and idea of the mothership "became a bridge between a missing African past and a glorious space-age future."[72] Along with Sly Stone, Clinton catapulted funk into the futuristic realm in which it still resides today, as many funk bands simultaneously pay tribute back to the pioneers while still propelling funk further into the future with sound and imagery.

Although Clinton is only credited on the opening track of *To Pimp a Butterfly*, his lasting influence on Kendrick and the other musicians involved in the production of the album is undeniable. Kendrick said in his interview with Rolling Stone that the album ended up with a predominately funky and jazzy vibe, borrowing from free jazz and 70s funk, because Kendrick was listening to a lot of Miles Davis

---

[71] Ytasha L. Womack, Afrofuturism: The World of Black Sci-Fi and Fantasy Culture (Chicago: Lawrence Hill Books, 2013) 57.
[72] Ibid, 63.

and Parliament.[73] Producer MixedByAli says that Kendrick works synesthetically in the studio stating, "he talks in colors all the time: 'Make it sound purple.' 'Make it sound light green'"[74] as Kendrick was sonically influenced by not only Clinton's funky sound but also his iconic otherworldly hair. On "King Kunta", one of the funkiest tracks on the album, Kendrick hits us with the funk so hard that we not only hear the music, but we feel it. As Clinton would say, the funk is already inside us and the music is just the apparatus from which we allow it to be recognized. There is a moment in "King Kunta" where Kendrick raps, "limo tinted with the gold plates/straight from the bottom, this the belly of the beast/from a peasant to a prince to a motherfuckin' king/bitch where was you when I was-/*POP*/(By the time you hear the next pop, the funk shall be within you)/*POP*." The *POP*s are interrupting gunshots hinting that now that Kendrick is the King, his life as become more dangerous and he will be the target for violence like other gangsta rappers. The track continues, indicating the shooter has missed, and the track turns the funk back on Kendrick's enemy. Just like George Clinton brought the funk down from the mothership, the funk brings a positive message and therefore can be used as a weapon against negativity and violence. The collective chants "we want the funk" call back to the roots of black music and identity, as it samples Ahmad's song by the same title and gives a nod to Parliament's "Give Up The Funk."

On the track "Hood Politics" Kendrick raps, "streets don't fail me now, they tell me it's a new gang in town" alluding to Funkadelic's 1978 track "One Nation Under a Groove" which contains the lyrics "feet don't fail me now". The "new gang" in town could mean the U.S. government working to systematically oppress black people, but that is nothing new. It could also mean that Kendrick is carrying on Clinton's torch and that he and his crew of Afrofuturist artists are here to extend Clinton's legacy of positive involvement in the African-American

---

[73] Josh Ellis, "The Trials of Kendrick Lamar," Rolling Stone, June 22, 2015.
[74] Ibid.

community, just a P-Funk did in the 70s and 80s. In the music video for "i", a preacher is shown stopping two black men from fighting and yells "Stop! Stop! We talkin' about peace! A piece of yours, a piece of mine, a peace of mind, one nation under a groove." The man is preaching for peace in the community and reminding everyone that they are simply one piece of the whole pie. "One Nation Under a Groove" is a clear allusion to Clinton and at the 1:10 mark of the video Clinton appears reading his own book "Brothas Be, Yo Like George, Ain't That Funkin' Kinda Hard On You? A Memoir".

Clinton's P-Funk helped bridge connections between genre's birthed from traditional African-American music like blues and jazz to the hip hop we hear today. Not only has producer Terrace Martin said that during the recording of *To Pimp a Butterfly* that they were listening to a lot of psychedelic rocker and Afrofuturist explorer of the cosmos Jimi Hendrix[75], but references in the album also help trace the generational evolution of popular black music. In "Wesley's Theory" the listener hears "Hit me!" a common allusion to a catch phrase of funk pioneer James Brown but also reminiscent of political activists and Afrofuturist hip hop group Public Enemy's track "911 is a Joke". Likewise, on "King Kunta", Kendrick calls out phrases "I'm mad" and "I can dig rapping" from James Brown's "Payback" (which the track also samples), while also referencing lyrics from Michael Jackson's "Smooth Criminal". By pulling from much of the history of popular African-American music, while highlighting the varying genres that make up that history, Kendrick is not only pointing to that which he has been influenced by, but also travelling back in the timeline of generational traditions and the ever-connected canon of black music in America.

Blues, jazz, soul, funk, pop, hip hop, and electronic music map how African-American music has continued to evolve and often become a dominant art form of all American art. Kendrick pays homage to this evolution by continuously alluding to and including influential and

---

[75] Andreas Hale, "The Oral History of Kendrick Lamar's To Pimp a Butterfly," *The Grammys*. February 15, 2016.

Afrofuturist artists who inspire his vision. In "Institutionalized", the listener can hear someone singing "zih zih zih zih" which is a direct nod to one of the fathers of hip hop, and founder of the Universal Zulu Nation, Afrika Bambaataa's track "Planet Rock", one of the first examples of Afrofuturist hip hop. Legendary singer Ronald Isley brings a rooted soul aspect to "How Much a Dollar Cost", "i" contains a sample of Isley's song "That Lady", and the video for "i" shows Isley picking Kendrick up in a car while Kendrick raps the third verse, acting possessed and alien-like, while hanging his head out of the moving car. On "i" Kendrick raps in a style similar to Afrofuturist icon Andre 3000, while Kendrick has also mentioned how impactful Outkast's influence was on the creation of the album. Stereogum's Tom Breihan writes of *To Pimp a Butterfly*, "to find another album from a rap star this clearly uncomfortable with being a rap star, you'd have to go all the way back to [Andre 3000's] The Love Below"[76] again pointing out Kendrick's hesitation with being included in the rap industry, but also his finding solace in Othering and alienating himself from the norm. Finally, "Complexion (A Zulu Love)" samples Big Daddy Kane's "Ain't No Half Steppin'" and features legendary Pete Rock, two hip hop artists who played an integral part in the birth of hip hop.

    The intent of including and paying homage to so many influential figures that shaped the musical landscape of America today falls in line with the Afrofuturism theme of pulling from the past to assess the present and imagine what the future holds. *To Pimp a Butterfly* highlights contributions from innovative figures like George Clinton to not only show how far African-American music has come in the face of industrial and cultural obstacles, but also to continue to blaze the trail of innovation and artistic vision for the generations to come.

---

[76] Tom Breihan, "Premature Evaluation: Kendrick Lamar *To Pimp a Butterfly*," *Stereogum*, March 17, 2015.

Past Meets Present: The Jazz of Thundercat, Kamasi Washington, Robert Glasper, Terrance Martin, and Ambrose Akinmusire

We've got a whole generation of jazz musicians who have been brought up with hip hop. We've grown up alongside rappers and DJs, we've heard this music all our life. We are as fluent in J Dilla and Dr. Dre as we are in Mingus and Coltrane.

– Kamasi Washington[77]

I want it to sound like it's on fire.

– Kendrick Lamar on TPAB[78]

After the release of *To Pimp a Butterfly*, Kendrick Lamar was called the "John Coltrane of Hip Hop" by Billboard. The album has also been criticized for not necessarily being a traditional rap album, with banging beats that you listen to while you roll down the street blaring it out of your car windows like the previous *good kid, m.A.A.d city*. However, as has been previously and will continue to be discussed in this project, *To Pimp a Butterfly* is intentionally *not* supposed to be a traditional rap album, but moreover it encompasses the wide expanse of African-American tradition, Afrofuturist musical influence, and the future of what hip hop music can be as an instrument of social involvement, political movement, and cultural commentary. Jazz is one of the earliest and most influential genres to embrace the Afrofuturist aesthetic which is not surprising as it embodies the essence of African-American art and, along with the blues, is one of the first modes of African-American music.

---

[77] John Lewis, "The new cool: how Kamasi, Kendrick, and co gave jazz a new groove," *The Guardian*, October 6. 2016.
[78] Ibid.

John Coltrane, who Kendrick has been likened to for his ability of pulling from the tradition of their musical styles and coming up with ideas that completely change the trajectory of the genre, was not only influenced and interested by the past traditional African music with albums such as *Africa/Brass* but also was obsessed with outer space, especially towards the end of his career, with albums like *Sun Ship, Interstellar Space, Cosmic Music,* and *Om*. This avant-garde approach as his career progressed made him one of the most out-of-this-world artists of his time and he left a lasting impression on not only jazz, but all genres of black music.

Likewise, jazz artists like Miles Davis and Sun Ra are considered influential figures in Afrofuturism. Miles Davis adopted an alien persona or multi-ego later in his career with bug eyed glasses while also mapping the connection from Africa to outer space with albums titled from *Nefertiti, Filles de Kilimanjaro, Tutu,* and *Pangaea* to *Sorcerer, Miles In The Sky, Star People, Aura, Dark Magus,* and *Agharta*. Ytasha Womack considers Sun Ra (along with George Clinton and Octavia Butler) one of the three pillars of Afrofuturism as the jazz artists claimed he was from Saturn.[79] These men are indeed not the only Afrofuturist jazz musicians but are a few of the most well-known and influential artists who pushed the boundaries of sound and visual aesthetics with their adventurous space and time travelling through the world of music. It is no surprise that Kendrick was delving into the discographies of Coltrane and Davis while he was writing and recording *To Pimp a Butterfly* and the result was not only a jazzy hip hop record, but also a similar exploration through space and time that linked the past of African tradition to the present state of African-Americans and into the future of African-American art.

Simply by looking at the credits of the album, a couple of the names that show up as producers and performers are Terrace Martin and Robert Glasper, musicians that are both rooted in jazz. Funky jazz fusion bassist Thundercat is all over the album, bringing not only his

---

[79] Ytasha L. Womack, Afrofuturism: The World of Black Sci-Fi and Fantasy Culture (Chicago: Lawrence Hill Books, 2013) 53.

aficionado musicianship to the album but also his Afrofuturist multi-ego persona. Winner of two of the most prestigious jazz competitions in the world, the Thelonious Monk International Jazz Competition and the Carmine Caruso International Jazz Trumpet Solo Competition, Ambrose Akinmusire provides the trumpet playing on the album. Guitarist Keith Askey, bassist Chris Smith, and drummer Robert Searight additionally assist in melding the hip hop, R&B, and jazz sound throughout. These figures play an integral part to giving *To Pimp a Butterfly* a jazzy and (dare I say?) sophisticated feel to the album.

Saxophonist Kamasi Washington exemplifies what modern Afrofuturist jazz is today. Not only did he win the 1999 John Coltrane Music Competition but shortly after Kendrick Lamar released *To Pimp a Butterfly* Washington released his own genre changing masterpiece titled *The Epic*. The almost three-hour album received rave reviews and ended the year alongside *To Pimp a Butterfly* on many year-end lists, while featuring a ten-piece band, a 32-piece orchestra, and a 20-person choir. *The* (aptly named) *Epic* is a creativity explosion of the history of jazz influence, as Washington towers over the album's sound and album art as the king of modern jazz, just as Kendrick proclaims to sit atop the throne of modern hip hop. *The Epic*'s album art shows Kamasi looking directly forward, saxophone strapped around his neck, wearing a dashiki, and floating in outer space, connecting African tradition with the outer cosmos, so commonly found fascinating by jazz musicians.

The Guardian considers Kamasi the modern "poster boy of this bilingual generation" between hip hop and jazz, a "love affair […] that goes back more than 30 years" citing classic hip hop artists Gang Starr and A Tribe Called Quest who were heavily influenced by jazz, as well as legends like the Notorious B.I.G. (who was mentored by a jazz musician) and Nas (the son of jazz musician Olu Dara). "A lot of us grew up playing with Snoop Dogg's band, the Snoopadelics"[80], Washington recalls highlighting their hip hop influence and background.

---

[80] John Lewis, "The new cool: how Kamasi, Kendrick, and co gave jazz a new groove," *The Guardian*, October 6. 2016.

Kamasi Washington played saxophone on *To Pimp a Butterfly* and conducted the string section on the album. He can be seen in the music video for "For Free? (Interlude)" again, wearing his trademark dashiki and holding his saxophone, representing simultaneously black music and one of America's truest art forms in jazz. Kamasi said the following about Kendrick on the track "For Free? (Interlude)":

> Kendrick, he has it in him. On "For Free?", the rhymes he's creating—when I heard that, I was like, 'Oh, so Kendrick, he's been into jazz for years.' I remember Terrace [Martin] told me that too, that [Kendrick] had just heard *A Love Supreme* for the first time. Like, that's amazing. Just because the rhythms he's putting in there are so perfect. I was like, 'So what does Kendrick play, bass? Is he a trumpet player on the side?'[81]

In an interview with Charlie Rose, Kamasi also compared Kendrick to John Coltrane saying his "music comes from another place".[82] About that other place, Kamasi also says that "jazz is like a telescope, and other music is like a microscope" hinting at the infinite possibilities both explored by jazz musicians like Coltrane, Miles Davis, and Sun Ra and still yet to be discovered.

In an interview with producer Rick Rubin for GQ Magazine, Kendrick related a conversation he had with *To Pimp a Butterfly* Producer Terrace Martin in the studio when Terrace recognized that Kendrick was greatly influenced by jazz without even fully realizing it. Kendrick relates the following about what Martin said to him:

> 'A lot of the chorus that you pick are jazz influenced. You are a jazz musician by

---

[81] Natalie Weiner, "How Kendrick Lamar Transformed Into 'The John Coltrane of Hip-Hop' on 'To Pimp a Butterfly," *Billboard*, March 26, 2015.

[82] Charlie Rose, "Kamasi Washington," *Charlie Rose*, March 18, 2016.

default. The way your cadence is rapping over certain type of snares and drums.' [Kendrick continues]. That's something just opened me up. And then [Terrace Martin] just started breaking down everything, just the science of it going back to Miles, Herbie Hancock. I'm listening to these chords, 'Man I like that sound what is that? [...] Oh, so that's what I've been liking all these years?' 'Yeah, you've been liking this for years. This is in your [Kendrick's] DNA, this is why you pick certain instrumentals that you pick.'[83]

The internal jazz influence from Kendrick's own upbringing and history of listening to a long lineage of jazzy music, once fully realized and harnessed within the studio, became the backbone for the production of *To Pimp a Butterfly*.

Channeling his inner Coltrane, Kendrick is seen at the beginning of the "For Free? (Interlude)" video leaning out of a window, wailing away on a sax next to an American flag and wearing a LA Dodgers hat, linking hip hop to jazz in a representation that America's greatest musical creation is black music. The camera pans down to a gospel choir while Kamasi Washington is now seen playing the sax next to Uncle Sam, a black woman, and Kendrick in front of a very large house, indicating that he has made it and has money, unlike many African-American musicians who were cheated out of their earning by record labels controlled by white men.

There are jazz elements throughout *To Pimp a Butterfly* as a result of bringing in the jazz collaborators to influence and educate Kendrick on the history of jazz. The jazzy outro to "The Blacker the Berry" can be read as Kendrick's admission of his newly discovered ties to his jazz roots. Producer Terrace Martin also compared Kendrick to

---

[83] "Watch What Happens When Kendrick Lamar Meets Rick Rubin for an Epic Interview," *GQ*, October 20, 2016.

Coltrane and goes further to connect *To Pimp a Butterfly* to Coltrane's masterpiece *A Love Supreme* when he said:

> I told him on a text—this record we're doing right now [*To Pimp a Butterfly*], this feels like your fourth or fifth record. It feels like your *A Love Supreme*. Like when Coltrane came to grips with the true spirituality part, and started giving up the horn technicalities and became deeply into the spiritual aspect, just getting really into improvising. I feel like Kendrick does this in his music. He is the John Coltrane of hip-hop right now. Soft-spoken, extremely humble, and the motherfucker's always practicing."[84]

This is extremely high praise, especially from someone who is versed in the history of jazz and the idea that Kendrick was somewhat channeling Coltrane in the process of making the album adds to the otherworldly feel of the work.

Washington does not stop with his comparisons between Kendrick and Coltrane. Regarding the jazz element in the background of "Mortal Man" Kamasi recalls, "we put one Coltrane thing on, and Kendrick just got it immediately. Like 'Yeah, that's it, because it's gotta be like fire.' That intense, 1960s jazz that people always associate with John Coltrane. That's what we were trying to get, because it felt like that, it felt like that time period when he came in, his energy. It just felt like the height of civil rights."[85] This is the most telling of all statements about the jazz elements on the album and a rebuttal to criticism that it is not a traditional hip hop album with club bangers and bass heavy tracks. The politicism of the current state of race relations feels a lot like that of the civil rights era and the album succeeds in recalling some of the musical influences that came from that time of heartache, struggle,

---

[84] Natalie Weiner, "How Kendrick Lamar Transformed Into 'The John Coltrane of Hip-Hop' on 'To Pimp a Butterfly," Billboard, March 26, 2015.
[85] Ibid.

and hope. The idea that Kendrick had this sense of 1960s jazz rooted in him and that once he was introduced to it he would understand and embrace it, shows that sense of activism and leadership ingrained in him as a spokesperson for his people through his music. A fire was lit under the jazz musicians who lived in the Civil Rights era and it led them to adopt an Afrofuturist aesthetic to take pride in where they came from and give hope for African-American's future, just as a fire was lit under Kendrick during his trip to South Africa to be motivated to make an album that took pride in his people, where he came from, and the struggle that black Americans have gone through, and continue to go through today.

Present Meets Future: The New Generation and the Electronic Music of Flying Lotus, Thundercat, and Pharrell Williams

The introduction of jazzy influence to the album came not only from the jazz musicians on the album but also from producer Flying Lotus and his longtime collaborator and jazz fusion/funk creature Thundercat. After *To Pimp a Butterfly* was released, Thundercat was profiled in Rolling Stone magazine which wrote the following:

> Beyond calculable measures, Thundercat shaped the sound of *To Pimp a Butterfly*. He'd pull up old records in the studio, furnishing an advanced-level jazz seminar for Lamar: Ron Carter, Herbie Hancock, Mary Lou Williams and Miles Davis. 'We went down some lines, a little bit of lineage. I [Thundercat] tried to inspire him [Kendrick] where he inspired me. […] I played him Miles Davis' 'Little Church' and he was like, 'What the fuck is this?' I was like, 'This is Miles Davis, man — and one of his baddest records.' He was always like, 'I gotta come to your house and take this stuff off your hands.'[86]

This education of the history of jazz allowed Kendrick to unleash the jazz influence that lived inside him and have a greater understanding and appreciation for what artists like Kamasi Washington, Ambrose Akinmusire, Robert Glasper, Terrace Martin, and Thundercat could bring to the album and his visionary future of hip hop.

    Although learned in the genre histories of the four pillars of Afrofuturist music jazz, funk, hip hop, and electronic, Thundercat and Flying Lotus embody the Afrofuturist aesthetic with their other-worldly and alien-like multi-egos. Flying Lotus, the grand-nephew of Alice and John Coltrane, often uses dystopian images in his album art, flims and music videos, while Jeff Weiss of Rolling Stone describes first seeing Thundercat by writing, "I first saw him about seven years ago playing bass for Erykah Badu, wearing intergalactic shoulder pads and an eagle-feathered Cheyenne Indian war bonnet. You couldn't tell if he was 23 or 230, the son of Bootsy Collins or Sitting Bull, a legendary session player or an Afro-Futurist anime hero."[87] The connections to legendary staples of Afrofuturist music Erykah Badu and the Coltranes situate these two anomalous musicians as the future of the genre and Afrofuturist aesthetic as it relates to expression in music, while Thundercat's father drummed for Diana Ross and the Temptations giving him an extra element of soulful genealogy. As the Thundercat profile explains, "the full scope of Thundercat's talent only became apparent after meeting Flying Lotus. […] It was Lotus who convinced Thundercat to sing, make solo records and eventually introduced him to Lamar."[88]

    While George Clinton and Dr. Dre act as influential mentors to Kendrick, and Kamasi, Ambrose, Glasper, and Terrace Martin give the album a jazzy-edge, Flying Lotus and Thundercat propel the album's sound into another galaxy and take hip hop, once again, into outer space. Afrofuturist artist Pharrell Williams, who started the record label

---

[86] Jeff Weiss, "Meet Thundercat, the Jazz-Fusion Genius Behind Kendrick Lamar's '*Butterfly*'," *Rolling Stone*. April 2, 2015.
[87] Jeff Weiss, "Meet Thundercat, the Jazz-Fusion Genius Behind Kendrick Lamar's 'Butterfly'," *Rolling Stone*. April 2, 2015.
[88] Ibid.

Star Trak, is half of the production duo The Neptunes, and part of the band N*E*R*D is involved in the track "Alright" and has been creating Afrofuturist music and making Otherness cool for almost 20 years.

It is no surprise that the "four corners of this [Afrofuturist] cocoon collide" on the first track "Wesley's Theory" and on the album as a whole, leading to ultimate reveal of the album; that the whole thing has been a time and space travel conversation with the one of the most influential rappers of all-time Tupac Shakur. "Mortal Man" is an over 12-minute track that uses an interview conducted two weeks before Tupac's death and edits it so that Kendrick can have a conversation with him, asking him a variety of questions about his life and career.[89] The piano playing in the background of the conversation gives a sense that the conversation is taking place in some other realm than our earthly one, possibly heaven or outer space. Throughout the album, with the inclusion of musical genres pulled from African-American history which represent simultaneously the roots of African music and the imaginative future of the Afrofuturist aesthetic, Kendrick Lamar and Co. create an album that is all-at-once classic, nostalgic, inventive, experimental, progressive, futuristic, and as we will discuss in the next chapter, relevant to the current state of political, social, and racial affairs in America.

---

[89] Music Journalist Mats Nileskar's November 1994 interview with Tupac Shakur for P3 Soul Broadcasting Corporation.

5.

The Politics of Always, Now, and Forever: How *To Pimp a Butterfly* Tackles the Past, Present, and Future of Racial Politics

But to call *To Pimp a Butterfly* a political record 'would be shortchanging it. […] It's a record full of strength and courage and honesty' but also 'growth and acknowledgment and denial. I want you to get angry — I want you to get happy,' […] 'I want you to feel disgusted. I want you to feel uncomfortable.'

– Kendrick Lamar qtd. in The New York Times[90]

An album released in March of 2015 couldn't have come at a better time to demand and grab the attention of the nation in terms of the racial politics that were and are at the forefront of America and the world's consciousness. With the rise in coverage and attention surrounding the Black Lives Matter movement, the end of the eight year Presidency of the first African-American President, the increasing video documentation of police brutality specifically against black bodies, the shocking statistics of black incarceration rates, and the election of a President who plans to usher in a new era of anti-progressivism in particular in regards to race, the nation is spending the bulk of the unforeseeable future debating and addressing racial politics head-on. Frustration, anger, polarity, confusion, transparency, hope and the absence of it, are but a few feelings of the maddening years the country has been through and *To Pimp a Butterfly* touches on those, and many more, in addressing the past, present, and future of racial politics.

The past contains the permanent stains of blood, sweat, and tears which will never dissipate as America was built upon racist

---

[90] Joe Coscarelli, "Kendrick Lamar on His New Album and the Weight of Clarity," *The New York Times,* March 16, 2015.

policies, not only taking the land we now know as our country from the Native Americans who lived here before the Europeans arrived to settle it, but on the backs of the slaves that were taken from Africa and brought to America to build structures, till land, pick crops, cook meals, rear children, be raped, experimented on, abused, and a million other demeaning acts that went along with a race of people being enslaved for hundreds of years in order for the country, ironically founded on the concept of freedom, to survive and ultimately become an economic, military, cultural, and political superpower. Without the free slave labor of millions of black slaves, the United States of America would not be the same country it is today, and the scars of that past will be continuously felt and addressed until the end of time, the shadows of the horrific acts committed to human beings, and the ideals instilled in those who thought slavery was justified, will linger through the generations, whether the majority of individuals choose to accept and acknowledge the aftermath of slavery or not. As political philosopher Noam Chomsky argued in The New York Times:

> We also cannot allow ourselves to forget that the hideous slave labor camps of the new "empire of liberty" were a primary source for the wealth and privilege of American society, as well as England and the continent. The industrial revolution was based on cotton, produced primarily in the slave labor camps of the United States. As is now known, they were highly efficient. Productivity increased even faster than in industry, thanks to the technology of the bullwhip and pistol, and the efficient practice of brutal torture [...] The achievement includes not only the great wealth of the planter aristocracy but also American and British manufacturing, commerce and the financial institutions of modern state capitalism.[91][92]

---

[91] George Yancy and Noam Chomsky, "Noam Chomsky on the Roots of American Racism," *The New York Times*, March 18, 2015.
[92] For further reading see also: Edward E. Baptist "The Half Has Never Been Told"

From slavery, to emancipation and the continuing black oppression, to segregation, the Civil Rights Movement, the first black President, the Black Lives Matter Movement and beyond, this is a country that will always have a history of dramatic and undeniable racialism that permeates through nearly every element of society.

The present status of racial politics in America is confusing, fluctuant, and frightening, as tensions are seemingly at an all-time high since the Civil Rights Movement. It seemed for the past eight years of Barack Obama's presidency, that there was a continuation of the undercurrent of racism in the nation, not only how his place of birth was called into question by "birthers" but how he continued to be called into question for his religious beliefs, despite no factual information to suggest he is anything but a Christian like he claimed to be. When Republican's gained control of the House and the Senate, they outwardly proclaimed they would do everything they could as a political group to stonewall any legislation the first black President attempted to pass. The way he has been treated, talked about, disrespected despite being the elected leader of the free world, is unprecedented in the history of American politics and the disrespect carried with it an undercurrent of racism, very rarely an overt admittance that it is because of the color of is skin, but it is undeniable there is one major thing that is different about this President which would cause an entire political party to cringe at the thought of him being a successful leader; that he is black. Obviously, this isn't a mentality and agenda held by every member of the party, and readers might even disagree that the first African-American President of the United States was treated any differently because of his skin color, but the underlying racist rhetoric, not only over the past eight years but since and before the Civil Rights Movement, has been apparent as a residual part of American life throughout history.

Now, with the equally unprecedented election of Donald Trump to the Presidency, the country has entered a new era of racialism in the face of racial political issues that have been a problem for many years. Now it seems that hateful racism, previously considered in large part as something to be ashamed of in public spheres, an ideal that was at the gentlest sense "old-school", and not to be celebrated, has becomes a source of pride for many Donald Trump supporters leading up to and after the election. Suddenly, people who were previously somewhat reserved publically in their brandishing of hate-fueled rhetoric, are seen wearing shirts and holding signs while screaming of white supremacy and generally having a complete and violent disregard for the humanism of other races. Indeed, there have always been individuals and groups that have been outwardly vocal about their racist ideals, but it has been decades since one of the core messages of a major political party, that is supposedly representative of virtually half of one of the largest melting pots in the world, is one of direct, unabashed, and unapologetic hatred towards African-Americans, Latinos, Muslims, and anyone else who doesn't represent the heteronormativity that has dominated political representation for hundreds of years.

This step backwards in the face of progressive ideals, the loud, often dominating, often unbelievable, and frightening shift from underlying to overt racist rhetoric in the political sphere is a blow to anyone who is progressive thinking. Often so unbelievable it seems laughable, until you realize that what is being said is actually meant, and what is happening is actually our new reality, the progress that has been made over the past ten, fifty, two hundred-fifty years is being shown to be minimalized in the face of unadulterated hate. However, in the face of this hate is hope. The hope that was felt when a black kid from Chicago was elected President and the hope that must be sustained to imagine a brighter future for our country for generations to come. The Black Lives Matter anthem "Alright" by Kendrick Lamar embodies that hope, in the face of violence and the odds being stacked against African-American individuals since they were brought from their home to be enslaved in this country. African-Americans have always and will always continue to prevail in the face of seemingly inescapable obstacles and Kendrick sends that message throughout the frustration and fear as he addresses the past, the present, and the future of what it means politically to be black in the United States of America.

Addressing the Caterpillar in the Room: Reimagining the Realistic Past of African-American History

A major element of the Afrofuturist aesthetic is acknowledging the cyclical nature of time, and that the past greatly affects the present and the future, but also the present and the future can drastically affect how we view the past. The white heteronormative has, until somewhat recently, been (often destructively) dominant in how America's past is talked about and even taught to students in school. Revisionist textbooks have become a topic of political debate, while often blatant misrepresentations of the facts are intentionally included in the teaching of schoolchildren.[93] The goals of this strategy could be to cloud or erase an ugly part of an historical record, or to shelter the youth from a violent or hateful past which continues to haunt the United States. This nationalist view is nothing new though, as revisionist history has been a part of written documented history for thousands of years. However, when a certain group or race of people has been largely in control of the revisionist history, other groups of people might be negatively impacted by said revision; their history, traditions, or cultures, either intentionally or not, altered in the face of subjective fact altering.

Also at the core of Afrofuturism—and a reason the concept came about in the first place—was African-American science/speculative fictions authors writing themselves into the genre and therefore into the futuristic consciousness of the readers. These authors had to do this to take back control of the imagined future which they undoubtedly would be a part of, but were not portrayed in, as the world speculated on what the future would look like. In a similar way, and to combat revisionists who were clouding a traumatic yet ultimately very important history of survival, perseverance, systematic oppression, family, community, and hope, African-American artists

---

[93] Laura Moser, "Texas Is Debiting Textbooks That Downplay Jim Crow and Frame Slavery as a Side Issue in the Civil War," *Slate*, July 7, 2015.

have written themselves *back* into the past of their ancestors to honor and embrace those painful memories which led to today.

Many African-American hip hop artists have understandably steered away from addressing this painful past to focus on more light-hearted themes of having fun and materialistic ways of life, but hip hop as an artistic mode of expression is not at all shy about addressing injustices from the past or present. Kendrick Lamar, as equal parts leader, activist, spokesperson, and preacher, uses *To Pimp a Butterfly* to embrace and celebrate the past that he and his ancestors have experienced. Often bringing up taboo or "politically incorrect" aspects of the United States tarnished past, both as a reminder and a proclamation that black lives matter, have mattered, and will continue to matter despite being continually and systematically shown and told they do not.

Straight from the first track of the album "Wesley's Theory", Kendrick acknowledges and alludes to the lesser known (or at least lesser discussed) idea that in the 1970s the CIA contributed to the crack epidemic which decimated urban communities by sending drugs and guns into cities like Los Angeles which escalated the problem.[94] This is an example of a potentially revisionist history almost like a conspiracy theory, but one way or another Kendrick wants the listener to think about how the U.S. government either directly or indirectly contributed to the problem instead of fixing it, ultimately leading to crime and drug problems that continue to permeate black and urban communities today. Reagan's "War on Drugs" has been proven to disproportionately target poor black individuals and by hinting that the CIA was directly involved in the increase of drug use in some of those black communities is a bold and aggressive stance, especially so early in the album. With "Wesley's Theory" the stage is set for Kendrick to hold no punches when it comes to assessing the history of his country and its relationship with the black community.

---

[94] For further reading see also: Gary Webb's "Kill the Messenger"

Also on "Wesley's Theory", Kendrick takes on the persona of Uncle Sam who is tempting him (a rich black rapper) into sabotaging himself by living an outlandish lifestyle and spending all his money to bolster and sustain the American capitalist system that thrives on the debt of its people. The song title "Wesley's Theory" alludes to actor Wesley Snipes' tax problem and that, despite being one of the most prolific and successful actors of his time, Snipes was still somewhat of a slave to a country that was built on slave labor. Kendrick is very self-aware of how consumerism feeds the capitalist system and keeps black and poor people "enslaved". Therefore, Kendrick lives a somewhat modest lifestyle, his most lavish purchase at the time of the album's release being a home for his parents. In "Wesley's Theory" Kendrick raps the phrase "before 35" playing with the idea that 35 is the youngest age that an American can be elected President and here he is indicating that he will likely be caught in a trap or scandal, like Wesley Snipes, before he ever has a chance to run for President. "Be*fore* 35" can also be a play on the number 435 which is the number of members of the House of Representatives, also a part of the legislative branch which historically and systematically enacts legislation which keeps young black men like Kendrick in poverty or in prison. Kendrick is aware that, if he is not careful, he could fall victim to the common trope in hip hop, and the sad reality of black youth, of dying at a young age.

Kendrick's character of Uncle Sam tempts Kendrick by offering him material things like a "house and a car" and "forty acres and a mule", treating Kendrick like a recently freed slave as historically, freed slaves were offered forty acres of land and a mule. This metaphor works doubly as Kendrick has made it in America and is "freed" from the struggle of the poor while poor blacks are still enslaved by the American Capitalist system and political policies. Uncle Sam also offers Kendrick a "piano and a guitar" representing artistry as an escape from being poor and black in America. The allure of the modern American Dream instilled in society by celebrity culture is ultimately fictitious and virtually unattainable. Kendrick draws parallels to the false promises made to freed slaves and the false promises of attaining financial freedom by becoming famous made to many African-Americans as they watch the small number of celebrities and athletes achieve their lofty dreams.

In another nod to the painful memory of slavery and Kendrick's apparent "escape" into freedom, he repeatedly proclaims "this dick ain't free" on the track "For Free (Interlude)". As one of the most recognizable moments of phrasing on the album, Kendrick again throws back to the slave days and the appropriation of black male genitalia. Unlike enslaved blacks, Kendrick's dick isn't free for the slave owners to do what they want with it, including breeding him so that their population of slave labor increases. He mentions that "matter fact it need interest, matter fact its nine inches" pointing to the historical fear of the larger-than-normal black penis in which slave owners and local law enforcement often would create false rape allegations that led to lynchings in which the black individuals would be castrated, hung, burned, and/or put on display for the town's people. "Matter fact it need interest" is Kendrick calling for reparations for these atrocities. Not only is his dick not free, but the country should pay him for the horrid acts that slave owners did to his ancestor's black bodies. Kendrick repeats "this dick ain't free" as an aggressive retort that he owns his body and his sexuality, which he is proud of as a source of power but also recalls a dark and troubling past.

The opening tracks focus on the historical shadow of slavery and the scars left on modern black life. In "For Free (Interlude)" Kendrick raps, "like I never made ends meet/eatin' your leftovers and raw meat" recalling that slave masters would give their slaves leftover scraps of meat and other foods which would later become what we now know as African-American soul food[95], what was once a degrading source of shame has now become as source of pride and tradition for many black Americans. This is one of many examples of the Afrofuturist move to reimagine African-American history i.e. taking something initially meant as something to damage self-esteem and

---

[95] Tim Grant, "Soul food: Scraps became cuisine celebrating African-American spirit," *Pittsburgh Post-Gazette*, February 23, 2006.

turning it into something that is revered and an important part of black culture.

  Even though Kendrick is seemingly "free" from the poverty/slavery of America, there is still the looming threat of America's past and present subjugation of black people through oppressive economic policies making it difficult for black individuals to succeed. Just as Wesley Snipes fell victim to Uncle Sam, Kendrick feels the immanency of the government's influence hanging over the success he has accomplished. Voiced by a woman, who throughout the album represents both the Devil (Lucy) and America, we hear her threaten Kendrick saying "i'mma get my Uncle Sam to fuck you up. You ain't no king!" indicating that the Devil/America is going to get systematic capitalism to keep him (the King of hip hop) down. This leads into the track "King Kunta" in which Kendrick fights back to proclaim he will not back down to his foes, the Devil and/or America. The video of "For Free (Interlude)" shows an old racist statue of a black figure with big lips that magically turns into Kendrick in the foyer as he chases after the woman. While he raps, fast cuts are made to multiple historically racist statutes such as monkeys and mammy figures, potentially indicating that Kendrick will utilize this racist history as a way to scare Lucy who represents America. The tactic of reminding the enemy of the hundreds of years of oppression and mistreatment should instill fear in America as Kendrick is now becoming a powerful voice and a formidable foe in the battle for justice and equality. Likewise, in "King Kunta" we hear a voice say "you goat-mouth mammyfucker" alluding to Jamaican Patois which says to be goat-mouthed is to be jinxed but also points to slavery and the racist imagery in entertainment of the mammy figure. The connection between Jamaican traditional lore and racist imagery is a message that the oppression of black bodies spreads far beyond American slavery.

  In "King Kunta", Kendrick references the "twenty million walkin' out the court buildin', 'woo, woo!'" alluding to black activist Martin Luther King Jr. and Malcolm X who spoke of the 20 million oppressed African-Americans during the Civil Rights era. As discussed previously, Kendrick strives to become a leader in the black community as influential as MLK and Malcolm X, as he speaks to the power of unity in the African-American community and the political, social, and cultural power that can potentially be wielded when all African-Americans bond together for a common cause. This is a sort of call to arms for a generation of black people that not only feel lost but disenfranchised within their own community because of oppressive legislative practices since the Reagan era.

In a 2011 MTV interview, Kendrick was asked if he thinks "that sense of being lost is specific to your [Kendrick's] generation?" Kendrick's response was this:

> There's a negative vibe right from the jump when you talk about [kids who were born in] the Ronald Reagan era, we was just corrupted from the jump. When I say 'Section 80,' I just speak on anything that starts from the '80s on up. It's always been a negative stigma as far as we don't have no sense, we don't have no morals, we just unruly and we do what we want. It just started from word of mouth and then it actually turned into that.[96]

Since Kendrick's *Section 80* album, Kendrick has expounded the cause of his generation's feeling of loss, especially on tracks like "King Kunta", further back into African-American history to include slavery, segregation, and the continuing struggle for equal civil rights. In the "King Kunta" music video pictures of MLK and Malcolm X are shown hanging from the wall as Kendrick raps "everybody wanna cut the legs off him" connecting his own status as King to the assassinations of the civil rights leaders he admires. The people that uphold the status quo in America want to cut down people like Kendrick who wish to disrupt

---

[96] Andrew Nosnitsky, "Kendrick Lamar Talks Rap, Religion and the Reagan Era," *MTV*, July 11, 2011.

oppressive historical practices and change the trajectory of the treatment of their people.

Kendrick is not shy about calling out those that uphold the status quo which keeps the African-American community from fully recovering from the stain of slavery, segregation, and unequal treatment. In the track "The Blacker the Berry" Kendrick attacks back rapping, "you sabotage my community, makin' a killin'/you made me a killer, emancipation of a real nigga." As someone who grew up in the 80s and saw a drastic increase in drugs and crime into poor black areas, Kendrick seems to believe the white-run CIA and the "War on Drugs" of the Reagan era led to the government benefitting from introducing a drug that led to an increase in black on black crime, a rise in the imprisonment of young black men and women, and a domestic social disaster purposefully brought on by the government in order to decimate the black community. This alleged "sabotage" is what Kendrick attempts to combat by exposing, revisiting, and reimagining the past in which he was brought up in, a past that shaped who he is today and how the African-American community interacts with the rest of American society.

Kendrick's Past

As is the case with many people who grow up to devote a portion their lives, passion, and art to being an advocate for a specific cause or striving to correct an injustice, Kendrick was undoubtedly propelled into his role as an activist voice in the African-American community by events in his childhood. As we see throughout *To Pimp a Butterfly*, Kendrick addresses America's past of police brutality, which has been a constant in black communities across the nation, but most recently has come to the forefront of America's media and political consciousness with the invention of camera phones that are able to capture unlawful acts of aggression by police officers on black bodies. The outcry and concern from people who are unfamiliar with the continued history of this unjust treatment is often voiced that this is an upward trend in police brutality, but it is common knowledge within communities that have experienced it for the past century that these acts by law enforcement are par for the course. It is the public exposure to the people outside of the community that is causing the current uproar and the need for activist groups such as Black Lives Matter and celebrity individuals to get involved and voice their own concerns.

In an interview in Rolling Stone, Kendrick remembers one of his earliest memories as one of police brutality and protest surrounding the Rodney King incident. He recalls, "the afternoon of April 29th, 1992, the first day of the South Central riots. […] I'm watching the news, hearing about Rodney King and all this. I said to my mom, 'So the police beat up a black man, and now everybody's mad? OK. I get it now.'"[97] This portion of the interview, and Kendrick's description of the events and the aftermath, as being related to a young child in its simplest form and the child's understanding of the how and why of the L.A. riots is telling. The simplicity of seeing the video of the Rodney King video and *feeling* that something is not right, despite the unavoidable outcome of some people feeling the beating was deserved, is ingrained in the memory of young Kendrick Lamar, but if that was the sole example that boy experienced, perhaps he wouldn't have grown up to be the man he is today.

In the same interview, Kendrick moves to his teenage years and his own interactions with the police saying, "[they] were not good. […] There were a few good ones who were protecting the community. But then you have ones from the Valley. They never met me in their life, but since I'm a kid in basketball shorts and a white T-shirt, they wanna slam me on the hood of the car. Sixteen years old. […] Right there by that bus stop. Even if he's not a good kid, that don't give you the right to slam a minor on the ground, or pull a pistol on him."[98] The feeling of not only fear of the police, but that you are being persecuted and

---

[97] Josh Ellis, "The Trials of Kendrick Lamar," *Rolling Stone*, June 22, 2015.
[98] Josh Ellis, "The Trials of Kendrick Lamar," *Rolling Stone*, June 22, 2015.

targeted simply because of who you are and what you look like, is undoubtedly a common reality for black individuals, especially in highly populated urban areas with higher crime rates. It is easy to imagine that in addition to the police unfairly targeting black people, part of the systematic reason for the disproportionate mass incarceration of African-Americans is that, like Kendrick, they are treated as criminals even if they have done nothing to deserve that treatment. The mentality for criminality is instilled in them at a young age. That is not to say that they are anymore naturally apt to commit crimes than young adults who are not treated as such by law enforcement, but that distrust of law enforcement and authority in general is not only ingrained in them growing up but can also be passed down through generations.

      Kendrick recalls having a police officer pull a gun on him when he was seventeen years old when he was riding in his friend Moose's car and they got pulled over. Moose apparently couldn't pull out his license fast enough for the officer and Kendrick recalls, "he literally put the beam on my boy's head. I remember driving off in silence, feeling violated, and him being so angry a tear dropped from his eye."[99] This all too common account is chilling with the recent barrage of traffic stops that have ended with black individuals shot and killed by police.[100] In the same interview, Kendrick goes on to call the police "the biggest gang in California" adding "you'll never win against them."[101] However, Kendrick believes he has found a weapon to fight against police injustice, maybe not to defeat the gang but to significantly injure it. In a XXL interview he said, "from 13 years old to the time I was 21, I was in a mode of mastering how to be a rapper. Like a rapper's rapper, using my tongue as a sword, a fuckin' barbarian. That's all it was about, slaying words."[102]

---

[99] Ibid.
[100] Amadou Diallo, Ronald Madison, Sean Bell, Kendra James, Eric Garner, Michael Brown, Alton Sterling, Philando Castile, Manuel Loggins Jr., and far too many more.
[101] Josh Ellis, "The Trials of Kendrick Lamar," *Rolling Stone*, June 22, 2015.

Ytasha Womack maintains that, "Afrofuturist music embodies the times while literally sounding out of this world"[103] and Kendrick's lyrics are representative poetry of African-American youth yearning for a positive voice within popular culture, and music that embraces African and African-American traditions while sounding new, exciting, and otherworldly. A major element and sustainable tool for the African-American diaspora to maintain strong cultural connections to the motherland is through oral tradition. Folklore, language, and spirituality found their way across the Atlantic and were central to the slaves because they carried memories of African heritage into the new and unfamiliar experience of a foreign land. Oral tradition allowed for that African heritage, through cultural retention, to be translated into cultural expression within their alien surroundings, giving the slaves a glimmer of hope and strength that helped them survive the nightmare.[104] However, as Kodwo Eshun argues, "the alphabet is not just a transparent communication but a ubiquitous technology, a system adapted and encrypted by successive religious regimes for warfare."[105] Historically, language through religion has often been used as a tool in which to enslave, demean, or exclude a group of people and as the African-American slaves were frequently punished for attempting to learn how to read or write, it is clear that slave owners felt that language could become a powerful weapon in the hands of their slaves. Language was not only a powerful tool for African-Americans to hold on to oral traditions and heritage but if a greater knowledge of the English language was established, ultimately it could be utilized to manipulate meaning and their understanding of the world, potentially leading to a revolt and freedom. As Eshun further argues, the prize of controlling or utilizing language is ultimately to control the means of

---

[102] "Writer At War: Kendrick Lamar's XXL Cover Story," *XXL*, January 6, 2015
[103] Ytasha L. Womack, Afrofuturism: The World of Black Sci-Fi and Fantasy Culture (Chicago: Lawrence Hill Books, 2013) 55.
[104] Roni Sarig, Third Coast: OutKast, Timbaland & How Hip-Hop Became a Southern Thing (Cambridge, MA: Da Capo Press, 2007) x.
[105] Kodwo, Eshun, More Brilliant Than The Sun: Adventures In Sonic Fiction (London, England: Quartet Books, 1998). 32.

perception, or in other words, for slaves to be able to read the Bible or write messages to one another on how to escape; they could then control how their enslavement was perceived by themselves and their fellow slaves.[106]

      Kendrick Lamar has understood, from a young age, the power of language and if, as Eshun contends, language is a weapon then hip hop is a type of warfare. In *To Pimp a Butterfly*, Kendrick wages war against American history and American government, the Devil, his own consciousness and flaws, and anyone that dares stand in the way of his message as the King of hip hop. In "Alright" he raps, "what Mac-11 even boom with the bass down" as police use guns as weapons against the black community, Kendrick uses the "boom" of music to fight back. The saying "the pen is mightier than the sword" comes to mind while listening to Kendrick's lyrics and watching him perform in front of massive crowds. The police might have the legal authority, but Kendrick attempts to capture the hearts, minds, and loyalties of his fans, and it seems that he may have the backing to at least stand up to the powers that be and represent the African-American community in its struggle for equal rights and fair treatment by law enforcement and the government. As a black man, there is no escape from systematic racism in America, and in "Institutionalized," Kendrick raps, "I'm trapped inside the ghetto and I ain't proud to admit it/institutionalized, I keep runnin' back for a visit". He can't escape the ghetto where he comes from, but he has found an effective tool for digging himself out of the economic hole many urban African-Americans are born into. Kendrick uses his past to show that there is a way out of the ghetto, but to stay rooted in where you come from is equally important as escaping.

---

[106] Ibid.

Ain't Nothin' Changed: Connecting the Past with the Present

The cyclical nature of time—connecting the past, present, and future—is again an important tool for Afrofuturist artists to express where African-Americans have come from, where they are, and where they are going often in the same idea or artistic breath. By using the somewhat metaphoric idea that African-Americans are still enslaved by America towards the beginning of the album, Kendrick raises the stakes of the urgency of social and political change regarding America's treatment of minorities. In "For Free (Interlude)", Kendrick's popular earworm "this dick ain't free" is repeated and is a play on words meaning he, as a black man with a dick, is not free in the sense of being a slave to the system that wants him to make music that is catchy with little or no substance. Kendrick is free and an artist with something to say, not willing to simply crank out number one hits with banging beats to get played in the club. After *good kid, m.A.A.d city*, Kendrick understood his greater calling as spokesperson of a movement and a generation even more clearly, so instead of following up his multi-platinum album with something similar that everyone expected and wanted, he instead put out *To Pimp a Butterfly*, a jazzy non-tradition hip hop album, which some hip-hop fans didn't quite understand right away or even at all, wishing Kendrick would conform to the genre.

Kendrick also contrasts forty acres and a mule to forty ounces and a pit bull to connect the past and the present while considering reparations. Forty acres and a mule was what some freed slaves were given to start a life post-emancipation while forty ounces and pit bulls are common things one might find in the hood. Kendrick could be saying that African-Americans deserve some sort of reparations because slavery has put generations of black Americans in a precarious hole since birth, and the government policies that have been in place for hundreds of years have kept many black people trapped in the hood, raising pit bulls and drinking malt liquor. In the opening chapter of her book on West coast gangsta rap "Nuthin' But a 'G' Thang", Eithne Quinn attributes the birth of the genre to a reflection of the dire socio-economic position many African-Americans faced in the late 80s and early 90s. Malt liquor, like gangsta rap, was something that the poor urban African-American community could call their own as Quinn writes, "this powerful, cheap depressant was the favored brew of young people with lots of time on their hands, frustrated aspirations, and little cash. Thus '40-oz culture' was a response or symbolic solution, as it were, to the problems posed by economic disadvantage and social isolation."[107] Again, Kendrick is connecting the current state of being black in America as a continuation of being enslaved and that reparations are not a sufficient remedy to alleviate the complex painful scars of that enslavement. In "Institutionalized" Kendrick proclaims, "Master, take the chains off me!" as he understands he (and his community) are trapped in a continued institutionalized enslavement based on the current state of America's complicated relationship with race and its treatment of black people. Kendrick's work serves as a protest against these injustices as he references the Alice Walker novel "The Color Purple" in the song "Alright" and echoes "all my life I has to fight, nigga," in concert with the Black Lives Matter mantra "we gon' be alright," indicating that Kendrick's struggle is that of many black Americans and not just his own. Kendrick aligns *To Pimp a Butterfly* with Alice Walker's great piece of African-American art and storytelling as he carries the torch of protest and inspiration through artistic vision into the present.

The Present State of Race in America: Black Lives Matter

I went to war last night
With an automatic weapon, don't nobody call a medic
I'mma do it till I get it right
I went to war last night (Night, night, night, night, night)
I've been dealing with depression ever since an adolescent
Duckin' every other blessin', I can never see the message
I could never take the lead, I could never bob and weave
From a negative and letting them annihilate me

---

[107] Eithne Quinn, Nuthin' but a "G" Thang (New York: Columbia University Press. 2005) 2-3.

> And it's evident I'm moving at a meteor speed
> Finna run into a building, lay my body
>
> - Kendrick Lamar on "i"
>
> For the past 96 years, "Lift Every Voice and Sing" has been universally considered the Black national anthem. Written by author/activist James Weldon Johnson and set to music by his brother John Rosamond Johnson, the uplifting hymn was officially anointed an ode for colored people by the NAACP in 1919. It's had an incredible run, but as Sam Cooke once sang, change gon' come. It's time for an updated theme song for Black folks. That song is Kendrick Lamar's "Alright". Hear me out. […] "Lift Every Voice and Sing" is peaceful and passive, but it's time for an anthem with a bit more bite. Imagine this bridge, chanted in unison: […] It's angry, reflective and real, but never loses that hopefulness. Plus a bonus dab of Malcolm X's "By any means necessary" mentality, for good measure. Because during the Eric Garner era, how many of us are questioning whether to reach for a Bible or a Beretta?[108] […]
>
> ["Alright"] has become our generation's protest song.[109]
>
> – Rick Rubin

In the summer of 2015 "we gon' be alright" became the rallying cry for the Black Lives Matter movement as they mourned the deaths of black people killed by police and hope for a brighter, more peaceful, future. Kendrick—along with many other artists, politicians, celebrities, and activists—was greatly affected by some of the early and more publicized killings of black men. The communities these men

---

[108] John Kennedy, "Kendrick Lamar's 'Alright' Should Be The New Black National Anthem," *BET*, March 31, 2015.
[109] "Watch What Happens When Kendrick Lamar Meets Rick Rubin for an Epic Interview," *GQ*, October 20, 2016.

were a part of were familiar with the history of police brutality and injustice that has haunted them. Police brutality and the killing of black people by police is something that has been a constant since slavery as some law enforcement officials have taken over where the slave owner's left off, demanding compliance with their demands and dealing out illegal physical harm and something death as punishment for not obeying. With the advancement of technology, especially hand-held devices being able to record the acts of violence and ideally assist in holding the offenders accountable if they act illegally, the media coverage and subsequent uproar surrounding the killing of black people by police officers has increased exponentially. Artists like Kendrick, and many other Americans, could no longer push these killings into the purview of their consciousness. As Kendrick relates, "I sat on the beat [for 'The Blacker the Berry'] and then the Trayvon Martin and Mike Brown situations happened and I knew that this needed to be addressed."[110] In his Rolling Stone cover story, Kendrick remembers channel surfing and seeing that Trayvon Martin, a 16-year-old had been shot. He recalls, "it just put a whole new anger inside me. […] It made me remember how I felt. Being harassed, my partners being killed," and he instantly started writing "The Blacker the Berry".[111]

    Kendrick's internal artistic call-to-arms in response to injustices of African-Americans in conjunction with the inspiration from his trip to South Africa and the work of Nelson Mandela are catalysts to the brilliance and almost universal critical praise of *To Pimp a Butterfly*. In an interview with The Guardian, Kendrick said of racial issues that have come to the forefront of political and social consciousness, "these are issues that if you come from that environment it's inevitable to speak on. […] It's already in your blood because I am Trayvon Martin, you know. I'm all of these kids. It's already implanted in your brain to come out your mouth as soon as you've seen it on the TV. I had that track way before that, from the beginning to the end, and the incident

---

[110] Andreas Hale, "The Oral History of Kendrick Lamar's To Pimp a Butterfly," *The Grammys*. February 15, 2016.
[111] Josh Ellis, "The Trials of Kendrick Lamar," *Rolling Stone*, June 22, 2015.

just snapped it for me."[112] Not only does Kendrick take on the multi-ego positive roles of preacher and spokesperson, or the mythical and symbolic roles of devil and America, but he also assumes the responsibility of martyrdom of the deceased Trayvon Martin. This mirrors President Obama's sentiments[113], and likely the sentiments of many African-Americans, that Trayvon could have been their son, their family member, or even themselves as the reality of the dire situation sets in. It is not that police brutality wasn't an important issue that needed to be addressed before, but the killings of Trayvon Martin and Mike Brown sent a shockwave through America and urged many people to finally say "enough is enough" and take drastic action to change the trajectory of America's future.

When asked about the high-profile killings of African-Americans by police in 2014, Kendrick said, "I wish somebody would look in our neighborhood knowing that it's already a situation, mentally, where it's f---ked up. What happened to [Michael Brown] should've never happened. Never. But when we don't have respect for ourselves, how do we expect them to respect us? It starts from within. Don't start with just a rally, don't start from looting -- it starts from within,"[114] which caused some controversy for Kendrick within the Black Lives Matter movement as the most effective way approach to activism was debated. Kendrick's call for self-accountability was taken by some as a generalized condemnation of the black community, while others viewed it as an accurate self-assessment and motivation to strive to be and do something better to help the African-American community. In their review of *To Pimp A Butterfly*, Pitchfork's Craig Jenkins wrote, "underneath the tragedy and adversity, *To Pimp a*

---

[112] Dorian Lynskey, "Kendrick Lamar: 'I am Trayvon Martin. I'm all of these kids'," *The Guardian*. June 21, 2015.
[113] Krissah Thompson and Scott Wilson, "Obama on Trayvon Martin: 'If I had a son, he'd look like Trayvon'," *The Washington Post*, March 23, 2012.
[114] Gavin Edwards, "Billboard Cover: Kendrick Lamar on Ferguson, Leaving Iggy Azalea Alone and Why 'We're in the Last Days'," *Billboard*. January 9, 2015.

Butterfly is a celebration of the audacity to wake up each morning to try to be better, knowing it could all end in a second, for no reason at all,"[115] as the album certainly evokes that emotion of uncertainty, panic, but also hope.

The rallying cry "we gon' be alright" simultaneously acknowledges the severity of the problem but also that sense of hope if the African-American (and American community as a whole) joins together to face those problems head on. Magazine NME reported:

> Kendrick Lamar's post-depression anthem "Alright" was chanted at the "Justice Or Else" Million Man March yesterday (Oct 10. 2015), with thousands of protesters joining in on a rendition of chorus line "we gonna be alright" in Washington. The march took place in celebration of the 20th anniversary of the original 'Million Man March', and took the theme "Justice Or Else". Nation of Islam leader and organizer Louis Farrakhan echoed the original calls from 1995, asking for social justice reform in America.[116]

In 20 years since the original Million Man March, many would argue that not much has changed in terms of race relations in America, with some arguing that conditions have gotten even worse, but in spite of the depressing conclusion that we might be going backwards instead of forwards in terms of how African-Americans are treated and their potential for becoming equally treated throughout all social realms of American life, the sense of hope continues to permeate movements like Black Lives Matter. African-Americans survived the atrocities of slavery and it is hard to imagine that the hope that is ingrained deep within the chanting phrase "we gon' be alright" will ever be extinguished. On "Alright" Kendrick raps, "I rap, I black on track so

---

[115] Craig Jenkins, "Kendrick Lamar *To Pimp a Butterfly*," *Pitchfork*, March 19, 2015.
[116] James Hendicott, "Kendrick Lamar's 'Alright' chanted at Million Man March for racial equality," *NME*, October 11, 2015.

rest assured/my rights, my wrongs; I write 'til I'm right with God" and he will continue to fight because he understands that legality and morality are two very different things in America.

For Kendrick, the future is something to strive for and be imagined, while people can only do what they can in the present to enhance their lives and lives of the people they care about. At the beginning of the first verse in "Institutionalized" Kendrick raps "life can be like a box of chocolate/quid pro quo, somethin' for somethin', that's the obvious". Kendrick understands that you never know what you are going to get in life, and in the face of positive advancement obstacles will continue to pop up to stymie that advancement. "Institutionalized" continues this theme as Kendrick touches on wealth's corruptive powers and violence brought on by the institution of money and capitalism which creates envy. Everyone is institutionalized in some way, the poor by the idea that success in a capitalist society is measured by the amount of money you have, and the rich by a fear of losing or someone taking their money or otherwise infringing on their success. The second verse of "Institutionalized" touches on the increasing income inequality as the friend that Kendrick brings to the BET Awards relates that he is fed up with rich people flaunting their money when poor people are struggling, so he decides to rob Kendrick's "co-workers". This individualized frustration, with income inequality, mass incarceration of minorities, police brutality on an unacceptable scale, and the general dissatisfaction with the racist underbelly of America, reached a peak of artistic expression at the 2015 BET Awards.

At the awards ceremony, Kendrick performed the track "Alright" on top of a police squad car,[117] directly linking the song's message of communal uplift in the face of unfair persecution to targeting by police. By standing atop the police car, Kendrick showed that a powerful message such as "we gon' be alright" is stronger than the individual members of the police force who engage in brutalizing minorities. This message of anti-police caused conservative media Fox

---

[117] "BET Awards: Kendrick Lamar Keeps Us Lifted With 'Alright'," *BET*, June 28, 2015.

News' Geraldo Rivera to say, "this is why I say that hip-hop has done more damage to young African-Americans than racism in recent years. This is exactly the wrong message."[118] This is an all-too-typical response to black protest, of accusing the victim of injustice of perpetuating it, but Kendrick's artistic message undoubtedly left an impact on anyone that watched it. Kendrick himself took flak from supporters of black civil rights when he called on black people to take more responsibility for the problems that face them, but Rivera's attack on his performance thrusting police brutality and the anti-police message in the face of the viewer caused Kendrick to respond. He said, "the senseless acts of killings of these young boys out there, this is reality, this is my world, this is what I talk about in my music. You can't delude that. Me being on a cop car, that's a performance piece after these senseless acts. Hip-hop is not the problem. Our reality is the problem of the situation. This is our music. This is us expressing ourselves."[119] Kendrick, as a black man and an influential artist, has the right to make a political commentary on the current state of race relations in America by utilizing his craft, but for Geraldo Rivera to attempt to argue what is or is not the correct message for a black artist to send to a black community, or the entertainment world at large, is out of place. Kendrick raps, "Nigga, and we hate po-po/wanna kill us dead in the street fo sho" and although this is a generalization of all members of the police force, he is simply reflecting the reality he—and much of the black community—find themselves in.

Kendrick's current reality is presented throughout *To Pimp a Butterfly* alongside reflections of African-American history and, as we will discuss later, the future of black people in America. In "Hood Politics" Kendrick raps, "oh, yeah? Everythin' is everythin', it's scandalous/slow motion for the ambulance, the project filled with cameras" pointing to the hypocrisy of street corner cameras allowing police departments to keep eyes on everything in the hood, yet it takes a

---

[118] Colin Stutz, "Kendrick Lamar Responds to Geraldo Rivera: 'Hip-Hop Is Not the Problem, Our Reality Is'," *Billboard*, July 2, 2015.
[119] Ibid.

long time for an ambulance to arrive if someone from the neighborhood needs it. It is scandalous that the government is so willing to spend money on incarcerating black people as opposed to helping them. On the track, Kendrick continues to tackle issues of hypocrisy and unjust use of force by police as he raps that, "the LAPD gamblin', scramblin', football numbers slanderin'". The police gamble with the lives of black people with their "shoot first ask questions later" mentality seen so often in the modern era, then they have to scramble to cover up their illegal actions, so they don't face legal repercussions. All the while, black people get arrested in disproportionate numbers and face "football numbers" which correlate to 3, 7, 10, 14 years in prison.[120]

      The hypocrisy continues up the ladder as politicians with more power than the police criticize gang life and criminal activity, all the while participating in corrupt and immoral acts on a national scale and affecting more people. Obviously, this is a generalization as well and not all politicians are corrupt, but Kendrick's message of hypocrisy along all levels of power and white privilege in America is still extremely valid. Black individuals face extended prison sentences for selling drugs, even marijuana, while politicians and bankers committing so-called "white collar crimes" that negatively affect millions of lives barely face any punishment more than a slap on the wrist. Again on "Hood Politics" Kendrick raps, "from Compton to Congress, set trippin' all around/ain't nothin' new, but a flu of new Demo-Crips and Re-Blood-licans/red state versus a blue state, which one you governin'?" making the connection that even the gang colors of the Crips and Bloods match those of the two main political parties and, quite possibly, in the minds of black America, those political parties are as damaging to the black community as gang violence and crime. Just as gangs introduce and distribute guns and drugs into the community, the conspiracy theory that the government did the same in the 80s to have an excuse to mass incarcerate black people carries the connection

---

[120] Common football scores equate to 3 points for a field goal, 7 points for a touchdown and extra point, 10 points for a field goal and a touchdown, and 14 points for two touchdowns.

further. Finally, the promises that gangs make to potential new members, of money/security/jobs/progress, mirror the promises politicians make to their constituents to get elected. By illuminating these hypocrisies, Kendrick is calling out and exposing the already apparent unfair and unjust treatment of black people and minorities in America. Kendrick proclaims, "I mean, it's evident that I'm irrelevant to society/that's what you're telling me, penitentiary would only hire me" indicting that the status quo is upheld when black people are removed from society, incarcerated, and ignored.

    Kendrick is aware of the power that his fame and critical acclaim give him every time he picks up the mic. "Conscious rap" is a label that applies to certain hip hop artists since the genre's inception, and Kendrick embraces the role as he says, "if you speak on this kind of subject matter you're labeled a conscious rapper. I don't even know [if] that word conscious can only exist in one field of music. Everybody is conscious. That's a gift from God to put it in my heart to continue to talk about this because that's how I'm feeling at the moment. The message is bigger than the artist."[121] In "Wesley's Theory", Kendrick is aware of his influence when he raps about guns, instead of glorifying a life of crime and bragging about being a "hard" criminal or thug, Kendrick is careful to highlight the painful realities and potential dangers of that reality. He uses the phrase "we should have never gave you niggas money!" from the influential "Rick James" sketch on Comedy Central's Chappelle's Show, a phrase that emphasizes the anxiety Kendrick feels about representing his community through is art. Rich and famous black people are often held under a microscope or held up as a role model in ways that their white counterparts may not and as Kendrick recognizes this hypocrisy, he embraces it as a chance to send a positive message into the community. However, there are always obstacles in the way of being a role model and spokesperson, such as "the Devil" and American political policies. In "For Sale?" he raps, "smoking lokin' poking the doja till I'm idle with you" as he

---

[121] Andreas Hale, "The Oral History of Kendrick Lamar's To Pimp a Butterfly," *The Grammys*. February 15, 2016.

understands that Lucy/Lucifer/America wants Kendrick to become idle, to not pursue his dreams of leading and influencing his people, breaking down barriers, and assisting in both a revolution and leading hip hop as a genre. The powers that oppose his goals want him to become idle or stoned and forget where his passions lie.

In the "For Free? (Interlude), a woman begins the track chastising Kendrick calling him a "motherfucker," a "ho-ass nigga," and repeatedly saying he "ain't shit" because he can't buy her certain things like a weave and a Brazilian wax. This woman represents distractions to Kendrick and how America treats black celebrities as simple and materialistic. The woman references her "other nigga" pointing out how quickly a new rapper can come around and become as famous as Kendrick, taking his crown as the King of hip hop. The pitfalls of inequality are the main motifs in "For Free? (Interlude)" as the woman expects financial support from Kendrick since he is famous and rich. Inequality regarding race and class is also alluded to on the track, as Kendrick references stereotypes of black males, slavery, and the presence of poor nutrition in low-income community.

All the obstacles Kendrick faces or has faced are common hindrances in the urban African-American community and they pop up as the walls in "These Walls". Kendrick says, "knock these walls down, that's my religion," indicating that with this album, he is attempting to break down the racial and socio-political walls that impede the success of black people, but also to knock down the walls of the cocoon of his fame that attempt to trap or pigeon-hole him as "just a rapper". Again, Kendrick is aware of the power and influence that celebrity gives him and the responsibility that comes with that sway. The rising pressure of being trapped inside the walls of oppression of America's systemic racism causes Kendrick to muse, "I don't know how long I can wait in these walls" but he is confident in his goal as he continues with, "I'd rather call on you, put your wall up/cause when I come around demolition gon' crush". Those that put up the walls of racial oppression will be demolished, for Kendrick's path and role is righteous and true, while the powerful weapon of the microphone and the public stage allow him the tools in which to defeat these obstacles.

One of the most important, frightening, and immediate modern-day obstacles for African-Americans is combating police brutality and getting to a place where they feel safe and protected in their own community. Although "Alright" has become the anthem for the Black Lives Matter movement and is generally a song of uplift and hope, the track is not shy about thrusting the stark realities of the current state of racial inequality and police brutality to the forefront of the discussion. Kendrick understands that black people are scared for their lives in their own communities as he raps, "but homicide be lookin' at you from the face down", possibly indicating that homicide detectives are looking at what the victims are wearing (i.e. gang clothes, or in the case of Trayvon Martin, a hoodie) to establish some justification for why they were killed. This line also evokes the image of a victim face down on the concrete, after being shot and killed.

In the music video for "Alright", Kendrick screams as we see a pair of shoes hanging from a telephone wire, a common sighting in urban communities and a symbol that can represent a few things. First, it can represent bullying as the person that threw the pair of shoes over the telephone wire could've taken them from a less powerful person and thrown them up there as a reminder of their power and the victim's inability to do anything about it. This can be a metaphor for police brutality in that the police bully black people who don't have the individual power to do anything about it, their pride out of reach, represented by the shoes hanging too high to retrieve. Shoes hanging on telephone wires are also an indication that drugs sales or gang activity are going on nearby or as a tribute paid to military soldiers who are shot down behind enemy lines.[122] This manifestation of human instinct to leave their mark on their communities and decorate their surroundings is also an attempt to remember and signify that someone has died. If the dead person's spirit returns, it will walk high above the

---

[122] See the Barry Levinson film *Wag The Dog*.

ground closer to heaven, so the people on earth throw shoes up there as a tribute to their death. These shoes will come in to play at the end of the video.

Next a young boy is seen skateboarding before disappearing and then reappearing laid out on the ground as if shot. Kendrick repeats the "misusing your influence line" of the poem that permeates throughout *To Pimp a Butterfly* as a reminder that the police misuse their influence and abuse their power. The dramatic and busy intro of the video shows scenes of police helicopters, violent men, a casket being burned in cremation, a crying mother or wife, a church, a burning vehicle, a crowbar breaking through glass, a man chugging Crown Royal, a Molotov cocktail, and men throwing money around under a bridge. As the same boy that was lying on the ground is now running from a group of police officers, another man is slammed to the ground and handcuffed, as if being arrested, then violently lifted off the ground as the arresting officer pulls his gun and fires in slow motion.

The scene shifts to Kendrick driving a car and whipping donuts in a parking lot, as the album track starts, and a little boy is holding and throwing down wads of cash next to him. Kendrick is shown floating through the air, giving (Black Power?) fist pumps as he hovers through the streets as the community waves at him. Back in the car, Kendrick continues to whip donuts around a police car that has three people standing top of it ala Kendrick's BET Awards performance of "Alright". The video has the same sense of community that mirrors the theme of the track as Kendrick is joined by a group of people chanting his song. This is similar to the "King Kunta" music video although instead of wearing his standard LA Dodgers baseball hat, Kendrick is now wearing a Chicago Cubs hat, possibly paying homage to another city were black on black violence and police brutality are most prevalent.

An officer spots Kendrick, gets out of his police car, and points his hand at Kendrick in the shape of a gun, representing both how easy and second nature it has become for police to shoot a black man and how childish the whole thing is. The white police officer has a shaved head, giving him a skinhead and racist look, as he pulls back his finger that acts as a trigger. Blood spurts out of Kendrick as he falls from the street light and again recites the poem reiterating the abuse of power by police. Kendrick hits the ground as if he is dead and the screen goes momentarily black, before returning to his face and showing him grinning at the camera, as if to say that "we gon' be alright". Kendrick recognizes that the message he is trying to send with the song and the video is extremely powerful as he smiles to the audience, even after such violent and troubling imagery which places the issue of police brutality at the forefront of the viewer's consciousness.

On the track "The Blacker the Berry"[123], Kendrick unveils and highlights some of the hypocrisies and problems with modern America's treatment of black people and African-American history. Kendrick raps, "been feeling this way since I was 16/came to my senses/you never liked us anyway/fuck your friendship/I meant it/I'm African-American/I'm African/I'm black as the moon/heritage of a small village" arguing that from a young age he participated in things like Black History Month, a forcefully politically correct fabrication of the celebration of black heritage, which rarely ever deals with real aspects of African-American or African history or current issues of racial inequality or divisiveness. Kendrick describes himself as "black as the moon" in that the true side of black heritage and black culture are never fully examined or seen in schools, just as the dark side of the moon is never seen. He sees this false acknowledgment for the political necessity it is and understands that it is not enough for the African-American community. He continues, "pardon my residence/came from the bottom of mankind/my hair is nappy, my dick is big, my nose is round and wide/you hate me don't you?/you hate my people, your plan is to terminate my culture" as he sarcastically apologizes for being black while pointing out that all people came from Africa yet African-Americans are the group that is held down and oppressed. The ambivalence of America towards black people works to terminate black

---

[123] Also, the name of a Wallace Thurman novel that shares some of the songs ideals.

culture, which is loved and championed for its creativity but also envied and hated because it is often much more expressive and celebrated than culture directly from a white dominated society.

Despite Kendrick's success in reaching the pinnacle of rap game and the music industry he still says, "I mean, it's evident that I'm irrelevant to society." This double conscious of success verse irrelevancy is a common theme in African-American expression. He is surrounded by a society built and sustained by racism that tells him he is irrelevant because he is black. He continues, "I know you hate me just as much as you hate yourself/jealous of my wisdom and cards I dealt" calling out racists who are the ones that deep down hate themselves and take it out on black people as he conversely loves himself (which we know he proclaims in the dichotomous track "i") because he has worked so hard to create his own success and hasn't let the "stacked-deck" system determine his fate.

In the third verse of "The Blacker the Berry", Kendrick loses control as his frustrations begin to peak and he goes off aggressively rapping, "this plot is bigger than me, it's generational hatred/It's genocism, it's grimy, little justification/I'm African-American, I'm African/I'm black as the heart of a fuckin' Aryan /I'm black as the name of Tyrone and Darius/excuse my French but fuck you — no, fuck y'all/that's as blunt as it gets, I know you hate me, don't you?/you hate my people, I can tell cause it's threats when I see you". There is a lot to unpack in this forceful statement. Firstly, Kendrick acknowledges that he isn't the only black man persecuted by American racism and that it is passed down from generation to generation. He compares the current state of racial issues in America to genocide, since the genocide of his people during slavery and the subsequent carried over racism in American, that still is apparent today, has also been passed down throughout the generations. That genocidal mentality can still be found today as we hear some Americans who still believe that slavery is a good idea and the police target and kill and greater number of black people than any other race. He again proclaims he is both African-American and African, showing pride in both identifications and contrasting the pride in his heart to that of an Aryan, hinting that the hatred he feels for the oppressor is just as strong as the oppressor's hatred towards those they oppress. He then mentions that he is as black as the name Tyrone and Darius, which are names that in our culture are identified as common black names but are actually from Irish and Persian origins respectively. This again points to the hypocrisy that most of Americans have roots somewhere else, and that instead of being a proud melting pot of different heritages and culture, the country has a continued theme of oppressing other cultures and heritages to support white heteronormativity. "Fuck ya'll" is Kendrick expressing his frustrations with America as a whole because of this hypocrisy and the whole final verse is Kendrick's peak of frustration with it all.

  Kendrick also understands that those guilty of the hypocrisy are not only those that consciously support the status quo which oppresses black people, but that his own African-American community is also to blame for the situation society as place them in. In the final lines Kendrick raps, "so why did I weep when Trayvon Martin was in the street/when gang banging make me kill a nigga blacker that me?/hypocrite!" The double consciousness comes to fruition as Kendrick calls himself, and his community as much of a hypocrite as the rest of America. Not only is this final line a reverse of the positive affirmation of blackness phrase "the blacker the berry, the sweeter the juice", but as author Michael Chabon points out, "Lamar's "I" is not (or not only) Kendrick Lamar but his community as a whole. This revelation forces the listener to a deeper and broader understanding of the song's "you", and to consider the possibility that 'hypocrisy' is, in certain situations, a much more complicated moral position than is generally allowed, and perhaps an inevitable one."[124] This goes hand-in-hand with the dichotomous track "i" when Kendrick proclaims, "I love myself!" which serves as an anthem of not only personal, but communal uplift in the face of systematic oppression. Just as the African-American community should be proud of themselves, their community, and what they stand for, they should also be cognizant of

---

[124] Found on the "The Blacker the Berry" annotation on *Genius.com*.

that which they do that upholds the status quo and assists in justifying the oppressive systems which they oppose.

In the next track "You Ain't Gotta Lie (Momma Said)", Kendrick explores rap and black culture by further rapping, "and the world don't respect you and the culture don't accept you/but you think it's all love". He speaks to the lack of respect the black community receives in the face of violent shooting deaths and the Black Lives Matter protests, even indicating that the protests themselves might make society respect them less than they already do. He continues to list emotions, repeating "complex" after each and indicating that he has fought though those emotions and both he and the black community often suffers from an inferiority complex in the face of racism. Sticking to the theme of the song, the loudest people (racists) are often the ones with the inferiority complex. Racism and hate cause everyone to feel inferior, both the oppressors, who believe that African-Americans are somehow making their own lives inferior, and the oppressed, who feel inferior because they are told and treated as if they are. He says, "so loud, rich niggas got low money/and loud, broke niggas got no money/the irony behind it is so funny" speaking to the influence of money in capitalist American and the pursuit of the American dream, that it is not enough to have money but you also must flaunt it, while everyone ultimately turns out to be the same slave to the system.

Kendrick continues this theme of mutual responsibility when he raps, "the truth you love to bend/in the back, in the bed, on the floor, that's your ho/on the couch, in the mouth, I'll be out, really though". The powers that be in both the music industry and politics don't want the truth, they want to pimp the truth and make it theirs (their bitch). This could also be attributed to those in the black community who ignore the issues in front of their face as not important or completely and unequivocally blame white heteronormativity for the position they find themselves in, not taking responsibility for their own actions. In the next track "i", Kendrick finds himself "in front of a dirty double-mirror" meaning that he has finally begun to understand his dirty double-consciousness, but also evoking that the double mirror used by police in interrogations is dirty and the police are crooked. The theme of this track is self and communal love, but to find that you must be willing to be true to yourself which is also the theme of the track "You Ain't Gotta Lie (Momma Said)".

Understanding the double consciousness, both positive and the negative elements of self, community, and society are what Kendrick is focusing on to advance his community and the country. Politicians, the media, and individuals tend to focus on the negative when it comes to race relations in America and although that is important, Kendrick sees a brighter future with his thematic proclamations of "we gon' be alright" and "I love myself". Once again, the fact that we have not only elected a black President as the leader of the free world, but also the fact that President Obama is influenced by artists like Kendrick Lamar, as proven by "How Much A Dollar Cost" being his favorite song of 2015, a track that highlights the economic factors of modern black oppression, are encouraging signs for the future. This shows how far we have come as a nation in regard to racial issues and how much further it is possible for us to go. The future is now and as Kendrick said after visiting the Oval Office, "I look at where I'm at today and realize that most of my success is owed to the mentors that was in my life. [...] I sat down with President Barack Obama and shared the same views. Topics concerning the inner cities, the problems, the solutions, and furthermore embracing the youth, both being aware that mentoring saves lives."[125] In "Institutionalized" Kendrick references a "presidential glass floor" which plays on the idea of the glass ceiling in that politicians and people in power can't understand or help the people beneath them because they don't understand how they are institutionalized themselves. Perhaps, the most powerful person listening to Kendrick's music and meeting with him and discussing the issues indicates that the future is in fact now when it comes to the politics of racial issues in America. One can only hope.

---

[125] Rolling Stone Oval Office

The Future is Now, The Future is Next

The cover of Lamar's second major-label LP flips that maxim with a fantasia of bare-chested young hoodrocks flashing cash and booze on the White House grounds, Amerikkka's Most Unwanted victoriously swarming a toppled symbol of pale-skinned patriarchy.[126]

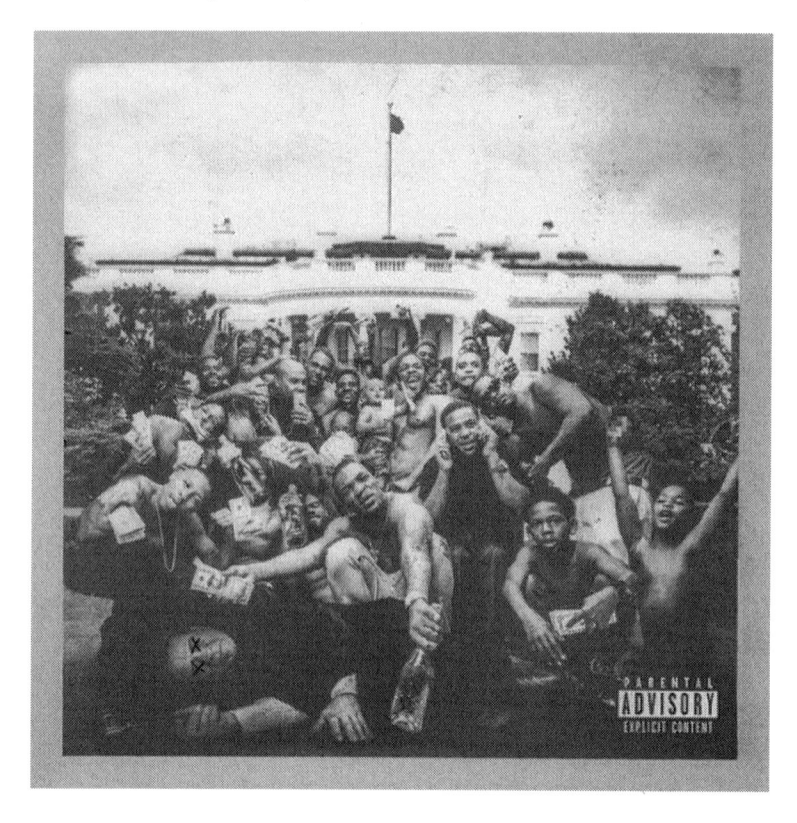

In front of the White House, Kendrick Lamar is shirtless holding a baby. Bottles of expensive champagne and booze are everywhere. Gold-chained black men, women, and children have wads

---

[126] Greg Tate, "Kendrick Lamar: To Pimp a Butterfly," *Rolling Stone*, March 19, 2015.

of cash, biting them with their teeth, holding them up to their ears as if they were a cell phone or a seashell, pointing them at the camera, as if to say, "Look at us, we've made it despite your oppression, despite your hate". They sit upon a toppled judge with his eyes X'd out and a gavel in his hand. The American system of [in]justice has been defeated, and what white supremacist America feared the most when Barack Obama was elected President has finally come to fruition. A young boy holds up double-middle fingers, on the White House front lawn.

Kendrick Lamar's stark album art for *To Pimp a Butterfly* represents that cyclical past, present, and future of the black experience in America. How far African-Americans have come to get a black man into the White House and to the most powerful position in the world, the current frustrations with the nation's justice system, hip hop's importance in American culture, and a "fuck you" attitude towards the future as if to say "we are here to stay and we aren't going anywhere. A change is about to come." The same oppressed group of people, whose generational past built the aptly colored White House which has been dominated by white men, are seen on the front step, knocking on the door to be let into and take over the political conversation. In a New York Times feature, Kendrick described that album cover as, "taking the same things that people call bad and bringing them with me to the next level, whether it's around the world or to the Grammys or the White House. You can't change where I come from or who I care about."[127] Thrusting the fearless imagery of what The Muse contributor Clover Hope calls "The Overwhelming Blackness of Kendrick Lamar's *To Pimp a Butterfly*"[128] into America's consciousness reappropriates and reassigns what the imagery of the White House means. These people aren't on the street corner or a dark alleyway shooting dice, they are as important as any person that has resided inside the building, and demand to be taken seriously.

---

[127] Joe Coscarelli, "Kendrick Lamar on His New Album and the Weight of Clarity," *The New York Times,* March 16, 2015.
[128] Clover Hope, "The Overwhelming Blackness of Kendrick Lamar's *To Pimp a Butterfly,*" *The Muse*, March 17, 2015.

This imagery can be found throughout the album in Kendrick's lyrics as well. In "Wesley's Theory" Kendrick raps, "I'mma put the Compton swap meet by the White House/Republican run up, get socked out/hit the Pres with a Cuban link on my neck/uneducated, but I got a million-dollar check like that" basically describing the album cover and alluding to the amount of power and respect he has in the African-American community. In the face of adversity and systematic oppression, Kendrick has literally reached the White House as he meets with and influences President Obama. The pimp, a symbol of the streets where Kendrick and the other people on the album cover have come from, has now turned into a butterfly and the previously labelled ugly, has become beautiful. In "Institutionalized", Kendrick even muses on what he would do if he were President, but that he is so institutionalized in the mindset of the hood that he would end up doing the same things he does now. In "The Blacker the Berry" Kendrick parallels his power with that of the President in charge of the nuclear codes as he raps, "and this is more than confession/I mean I might press the button just so you know my discretion". He is threatening to push the button—to drop the bomb or start the record—and let everyone know what his goals are; to challenge racism and oppression and be the spokesperson for the African-American community.

At the 2016 Grammys, Kendrick performed "The Blacker the Berry" and "Alright". Coming out dressed as a prisoner and part of a chain gang with other black people, the stark symbolic message on the mass incarceration of black people in America is sent from the start. As he aggressively raps "The Blacker the Berry" the camera pans over some white faces in the crowd who look confused and in shock, a powerful reminder that Kendrick is not only unafraid to send a strong political message, but is unabashed at doing it on the biggest stage in music, with little to no regard for the fragile sensibilities of the people in the crowd whose lives are as far removed from the streets of Compton as they can possibly be. Kendrick then stumbles over to another stage setting where he performs "Alright" with a raging fire behind him, possibly a call to action in the form of riotous revolution. The whole thing is quite dream-like as the camera makes fast cuts and Kendrick raps accurate and aggressively. Kendrick even added a new verse at the end of "Alright" about modern slavery in memory of Trayvon Martin stating, "On February 26th I lost my life too". This performance brought the racial and political frustrations to the forefront of the entertainment industry's consciousness, making it impossible for the music industries' elite to stand idley and comfortably by while police brutality and mass incarceration of African-Americans were happening all over the country. The Black Lives Matter movement brought the conversation to the political world, and Kendrick had now thrust it into the entertainment world.

In the music video for "For Free? (Interlude)", Kendrick is seen chasing the woman (Lucy/America) and frightening her. He is then seen dressed up as Uncle Sam, shoveling coal into the furnace of the house, a metaphor for America fanning the flames of systematic racism. Kendrick is also chasing and scaring the woman to challenge her. When she believes she has escaped the house and Kendrick, she finds the driveway where a dozen Kendrick's are, playing croquet, driving a minivan, trimming hedges, reading under a tree, and eating hor d'oeuvres and drinking champagne. Basically, all these multi-egos of Kendrick are seen doing traditionally rich white people things because he has finally made it professionally and financially and he can ruffle the feathers of those that sustain the status quo of white socio-economic dominance.

This push for change and challenging the current state of racial affairs is prevalent throughout the album, the accompanying music videos and visual art. The video for "Alright" is completely black and white, possibly pointing to the stark binary difference of what it means to be black or white in America when it comes to how the police treat a person. The opening scene is desolate and almost post-apocalyptic as if to say that things need to change soon, or this is how the future is going to look. A man in the backseat of the car pours out malt liquor for his dead homies (possibly at the hands of the police) as the camera pans out and we see that the car is being carried by four police officers. Kendrick and his boys are now seen as royalty and the police officers as the slaves in a drastic flip flop of the past/present and the future. In "i" Kendrick proclaims, "how many times the city making me promises?/So I promise this, nigga" referencing that the "city" or government promises the American dream in the form of jobs or social and communal uplift but rarely delivers on that promise to the lower-class communities. Kendrick promises to come through and uplift their future through the powerful message of self-love and acceptance.

Finally, in "Mortal Man," Kendrick imagines his own future (in which the powers that be conspire against him), his promises to his community, and his message to the African-American community. He raps, "if I'm tried in a court of law, if the industry cut me off/if the government want me dead, plant cocaine in my car/would you judge me a drug-head or see me as K. Lamar/or question my character and degrade me on every blog". Kendrick doesn't do drugs, so he imagines a conspiracy situation in which the government attempts to try to tarnish what he is trying to do. Kendrick has seen many powerful black men fall, by scandal and assassination, just when they are reaching the peak of their influence on society, but by being cognizant of the history of those that came before him and being aware of the pitfalls and obstacles that will try to derail his goals, he has a better chance of avoiding them. Kendrick uses the Afrofuturist technique of pulling from the past to imagine the future, to learn and use what has happened in the past to propel his goals.

Pulling from the Past to Imagine the Future: An Afrofuturist's Guide

> Wouldn't you know/we been hurt, been down before/nigga, when our pride was low/lookin' at the world like, "Where do we go?"
>
> – Kendrick Lamar on "Alright"

> That's how I see it, my word is bond. I see--and the ground is the symbol for the poor people, the poor people is gonna open up this whole world and swallow up the rich people. Cause the rich people gonna be so fat, they gonna be so appetizing, you know what I'm saying, wealthy, appetizing. The poor gonna be so poor and hungry, you know what I'm saying it's gonna be like... there might be some cannibalism out this mutha, they might eat the rich.
>
> – Tupac Shakur on "Mortal Man"

As we have discussed in previous section, one of the most important motives of Afrofuturist artists is to insert themselves and black people into representations of the future of which they will play an integral part. There are many ways to do this, involving being able to assess the situations, cause and effect, and historical relevance of African-American culture or, in other words, by pulling from the past to imagine the future. Culture and tradition, despite being nearly wiped out by slavery, are an important source of pride for African-American communities as they can point to their unbelievable will to survive in looking towards what the future has in store for them as a people. This pulling from the past is also important in assessing the current racial and political state of America and that, if African-Americans can survive the atrocities of slavery and integrate as equal members of society, then they can surely overcome the obstacles and unfair treatment they often face today. "Alright" sends that message. It explores the psychological concerns of being black in America and the feeling of displacement from being part of the African Diaspora and not quite being fully accepted by a significant percentage of the people in the U.S., who continuously vote, protest, or participates in racist rhetoric which is destructive to the advancement of black people. The pride and frustration are a result of hundreds of years of oppression, but also a source of motivation and hope which allows generations of black people to look forward to a brighter future.

Kendrick is part of a rap collective called Black Hippy, a name which pays homage to the importance of the hippie movement as an avenue for political change through positive messages of protest. Along with rappers Ab-Soul, Jay Rock, and Schoolboy Q, these rappers are inspired by the communal effectiveness of the hippies in the late 60s and 70s and could be naming themselves after that as a way to channel that activist traditional past in order to use their artistry in positive way to make the future a better place. This push for civil and human rights is obviously prevalent theme throughout the album and when Kamasi Washington was asked about this influence he said about "Mortal Man", "we put one Coltrane thing on, and Kendrick just got it immediately. Like 'Yeah, that's it, because it's gotta be like fire.' That intense, 1960s jazz that people always associate with John Coltrane. That's what we were trying to get, because it felt like that, it felt like that time period when he came in, his energy. It just felt like the height of civil rights."[129] Black Hippy, 60s jazz, social protest, all bring that all so important time in black and American history to the present, in an album that sounds like and has an energy like it is from the future. This push for equality and change isn't solely the responsibility of the black community, although Kendrick consistently alludes to the importance of black people working together, but in "Hood Politics" Kendrick uses a sample of "All for Myself", a song written and performed by indie artist Sufjan Stevens, a nod to the hippy and civil rights movements which were successful in inducing change with a collective effort from passionate people from all races and backgrounds.

In "Complexion (A Zulu Love)" Kendrick imagines a world where skin color doesn't matter. He alludes to slavery when he brings up the difference in skin color between house and "field niggas" when he says he needs to be snuck through the back door because he is too black to be in the house. He makes "a flower for you outta cotton just to chill with you" and "you know I'd go the distance, you know I'm ten

---

[129] Natalie Weiner, "How Kendrick Lamar Transformed Into 'The John Coltrane of Hip-Hop' on 'To Pimp a Butterfly," *Billboard*, March 26, 2015.

toes down" as he is willing to be physical mutilated to go through the danger of spending time with a house slave he describes as having blue eyes and light skin. In the slave days, a black woman with light-skin usually meant that her mother was raped by a slave master as he says "your blue eyes tell me your mama can't run". This separation of African-Americans based on the shade of their blackness alludes to the William Lynch theory that "the best way of controlling slaves is to exploit differences, such as age or skin color, between the slaves. By focusing on these differences, the slave owner pits slaves with dissimilar backgrounds or complexions against each other, rather than together against the owner."[130] Unity despite what your complexion is in imperative against opposing forces and has been for hundreds of years.

      We also hear the first female perspective on the album during "Complexion (A Zulu Love)" (unless you consider "Lucy") as the prominent rapper, and member of the Universal Zulu Nation, Rapsody appears on the track. She continues Kendrick's theme of travelling through time to connect the slave days to modern times by rapping, "all my solemn men up north, twelve years a slave" which is a play on Solomon Northrup (the author of the slave memoir Twelve Years a Slave) while alluding to slavery and a salute to black men who have been "sent up North" to the penitentiary and are in prison. The allusion to *Twelve Years a Slave* connects the 1800s to modern times by indicting that the Northrup's story is still as relevant today as it was when it was written, as seen by the recognition of the 2013 film winning the Academy Award for Best Picture. The salute to black men that have been imprisoned and comparing the mass incarnation of black men as another form of slavery continues *To Pimp a Butterfly*'s motif of connecting modern day racial issues to the formation of this country built upon the backs of slave labor. Rapsody continues, "ain't no stress, jigga boos wanna be/I ain't talkin' Jay, I ain't talkin' Bey/I'm talkin' days we got school watchin' movie screens/and spike your self-esteem/the

---

[130] Willie Lynch, "The Willie Lynch Letter: The Making Of A Slave!," December 25, 1712.

new James Bond gon' be black as me" to point out that there are important and powerful black figures and black people have nothing to be ashamed of when they have people like Jay-Z and Beyoncé to look up to, and the next James Bond is rumored to be a black man (Idris Elba).[131]

Just as "u" and "i" serve has song counterparts, "Complexion (A Zulu Love)" and "The Blacker the Berry" share a double consciousness of the album to point out that although the color of a person's skin is meaningless in regard to negativity and race is a social construct, it can still be utilized as a source of pride and community and as a positive identity marker. In "Hood Politics" Kendrick raps, "Everybody want to talk about who this and who that/who the realest and who wack, or who white or who black" as he feels that rap beefs and gossip are insignificant just like it doesn't (or shouldn't) matter what skin color you are. However, as is obvious within the current socio-political landscape, race is one of the most important and talked about subjects of our time. In "The Blacker the Berry" Kendrick describes a riot scene expressing the frustrations of black people over systemic oppression based on race. He says, "burn, baby, burn" which was the rally cry for the 1965 Watts riots, an important moment in African-American history of urban unrest which seems to be what Kendrick's message is of the urban unrest in the 21st century. Kendrick begins each verse of the song from the point of view of a black person frustrated and enraged at the commonality of police brutality and unfair treatment by the many branches of government.

One way artists combat the status quo of racial persecution is to break down or flip the negative connotations of stereotypes that have permeated culture and are destructive to their identity. In "The Blacker the Berry" Kendrick wishes to redefine negative associations with being black as he says he is "a proud monkey" and that he has made it despite systematic racism in America. All odds were against him and he has succeeded, so he embraces the identity marker of monkey and uses it as

---

[131] Seth Kelley, "Idris Elba Calls James Bond Casting 'The Wildest Rumor in the World'," *Variety*, July 22, 2016.

a word of empowerment. Also in "The Blacker the Berry" Kendrick expresses pride in beating a game rigged against black men like him as he raps, "and man a say they put me inna chains, cah' we black/imagine now, big gold chains full of rocks/how you no see the whip, left scars pon' me back/but now we have a big whip parked pon' the block". He contrasts the chains of slavery to the gold chains with rocks (diamonds) rappers wear as a marker of this affluence and success in the music industry and the whips used to punish slaves to the multiple whips (cars) he can afford.

Possibly the most powerful word in African-American culture is "Nigger" or, more commonly used in rap lyrics, "Nigga". In "i" Kendrick mentions the negative context of the word "nigga" and compares using it to being no better than Samuel L. Jackson's character Stephen in the Quentin Tarentino film *Django Unchained*. He raps, "I promised Dave I'd never use the phrase 'fuck nigga'/he said, 'Think about what you saying: 'Fuck niggas'/no better than Samuel on Django/no better than a white man with slave boats" as a way to argue that saying "fuck niggas" or "fuck black men" and embracing that word's negative connotation is helping keep black people oppressed and enslaved within the system. Kendrick goes on to try to change the connotation of nigga, by explaining how the word "negus" could replace "nigga" and become a source of empowerment and pride. He name drops Oprah and says "So I'ma dedicate this one verse to Oprah/on how the infamous, sensitive N-word control us" as Oprah is outspoken about the word "nigga".[132] He continues, "well, this is my explanation straight from Ethiopia/N-E-G-U-S definition: royalty; King royalty - wait listen/N-E-G-U-S description: Black emperor, King, ruler, now let me finish/the history books overlook the word and hide it/America tried to make it to a house divided/the homies don't recognize we been using it wrong/so I'ma break it down and put my game in a song/N-E-G-U-S, say it with me." This verse is Kendrick's attempt to redefine black history and rhetoric, turning a destructive,

---

[132] Katherine Heintzelman, "Oprah Winfrey, Forest Whitaker Talk *Lee Daniels' The Butler*, Racism, and the N-word," *Parade*, July 21, 2013.

hurtful, and historically sensitive word like "nigga" into something to be proud of, an identification of power, leadership, and the true history that white America has attempted to erase from their culture and history books. "America tried to make it to a house divided" is a reference to President Lincoln's famous "House Divided" speech to unite the black community. Lincoln said, "A house divided against itself cannot stand. I believe this government cannot endure, permanently, half slave and half free. I do not expect the Union to be dissolved — I do not expect the house to fall — but I do expect it will cease to be divided", which seems to run parallel with part of Kendrick's message throughout *To Pimp a Butterfly*.

    We see this message in visual representations of the album like in the music video for the track "i". The opening shows black people in a club, dancing and having fun. Kendrick is getting his nappy hair braided while women caress their bodies and freely enjoy themselves. Two men are seen wrestling; a cord is unplugged from the amp, stopping the music. Two police are seen arresting a black man as he walks through the scene and continues running with the community behind him. He walks by what looks to be a domestic violence scene about to occur, further pressing the message of black unity, how black people can't fight amongst themselves, and the problem with disrespecting black women. These scenes of stereotypical urban black problems can be solved by self-love and community, the message of the track "i".

    Finally, these socio-political themes all come to a head in the last track "Mortal Man" where it is revealed that the entire album has been an internalized conversation with the deceased Tupac Shakur. Kendrick uses Tupac to imagine the future and possible solutions to present problems within the African-American community. Kendrick finishes the poem, which resonates throughout the album, and it is revealed that he has been reading it to Tupac. Of the poem, Kendrick said in an interview for GQ with Rick Rubin, "[The poem idea] came in the process of me actually recording the records. I wanted a thread that conceptually tied in the songs. I've just always been a fan of movie flicks and writers. I just love writers man."[133] Rubin goes on to explain that sometimes when he is listening to *To Pimp a Butterfly* and he hears the poem being recited that he thinks the record messed up and went back to an earlier part. He notes that the poem takes you out of the album yet also ties it together and this is yet another example of time travel, where the poem makes the listener feel like they are somewhere along the timeline of the album that they are not. The poem ends with the lines, "forgetting all the pain and hurt we caused each other in these streets/if I respect you, we unify and stop the enemy from killing us/but I don't know, I'm no mortal man, maybe I'm just another nigga." Kendrick's brain has clearly been sparked, by his trip to South Africa, by the current state of racial issues in America, and by the inspiration that revolutionary black figures from Nelson Mandela to Tupac have given him. It is now Kendrick's turn to spark the minds of the youth for long-term change into the future. During their mythical conversation, Tupac mentions the frustration of socio-economical and racial difference, which unfortunately hasn't gotten any better in Kendrick's modern time. His "eat the rich" statement, quoted in the epigraph of this section, seems prophetical and current in that if he was saying the same thing in 2016, many people would agree. Kendrick isn't quite as pessimistic as Tupac and perhaps that is because he sees positive indications of change for the future.

---

[133] "Watch What Happens When Kendrick Lamar Meets Rick Rubin for an Epic Interview," *GQ*, October 20, 2016.

6.

God Is Gangsta: The Religion of *To Pimp a Butterfly*

[Kendrick Lamar]

And through your different avenues of success, how would you say you managed to keep a level of sanity?

[Tupac Shakur]

By my faith in God, by my faith in the game, and by my faith in "all good things come to those that stay true." You know what I'm saying, and it was happening to me for a reason, you know what I'm saying, I was noticing, shit, I was punching the right buttons and it was happening.[134]

Never shying away from the pride, he takes in being a spiritual and religious man, Kendrick Lamar places a great deal of responsibility for his success, both in the music industry and battling his inner demons, to his faith in God. Just as African-Americans blended their own cultural belief systems, carried over from their home land, with euro-centric Christianity adopted during colonization, Kendrick uses his own religious beliefs as a source of power to get him through tough situations and internal struggles. Belief in God has been a staple of community and an avenue of hope that things will get better in the future for African-Americans since and during slavery. Kendrick, via his conversation with Tupac (which may or may not take place in an otherworldly spiritual realm) gains inspiration from his faith, allowing him comfort in taking the metaphorical role of preacher, savior, and simply believer in his metaphysical battle against Lucy/Lucifer.

As has been the case throughout this project, the past, present, and future are connected cyclically, and the religious elements of the

---

[134] "Mortal Man"

album are no different. Kendrick pulls from the past of African-American and American culture of religion to allude to the strength and power that a beaten down group of people can summon if they have a faith in a higher power which unifies them. There are allusions to stories and symbols from the Bible which guide him through his struggle, as he finds solace and wisdom in the past to address not only his internal struggles, but those of the African-American community. His resistance against Lucy/Lucifer and everything represented by the evils in this world take place in Kendrick's present as the album takes us through the ups and downs he faces and he succeeds professionally, learning more about himself and his identity as an African-American man, an artist, and a leader. The present leads to the future and the addresses the questions of what is in store for Kendrick and the African-American community within a nation that continues to systematically oppress them and elect politicians that promote overt and unapologetic racism in a country seemingly divided by white nationalist ideals.

To Battle the Devil, You Better Have Some Power

Just as is the case in an uncountable number of works of art in human history, the protagonist (Kendrick) parallels or can be analytically compared to Jesus Christ. *To Pimp a Butterfly* is no different. The album was inspired by Kendrick's trip to Africa where he got in touch with not only his ancestral roots but the roots of all mankind. However, Kendrick himself might argue against this comparison as he is very much ingrained in his human experience and he even raps in King Kunta, "if these walls could talk they'd tell me to swim good/no boat, I float better than he would/no life jacket, I'm not the God of Nazareth". Kendrick can't walk on water like Jesus could, he understands his limitations and that he won't be able to perform miracles, however, his conscious tells him to "swim good" and try his best. This is where Kendrick finds his inner Christ, his inner Mandela, his inner Tupac, or whomever he is inspired by, in using the gifts he has been given helping those that are less fortunate, disrupting the authoritative status quo, and challenging those who abuse power and justice to oppress groups of people. He is Christ-like in his actions, humble but proud in his approach, and conscientious of what he can and cannot control.

Kendrick knows that he's not perfect like Jesus, but a sinner like the rest of us. In an interview with MTV News he said the following:

> I wouldn't say I'm the most religious person, neither were both of my parents. I always do quote-unquote religious songs or whatever you want to call them from the standpoint where I'm trying to find answers. That's the space I speak from and a lot of people can relate because they feel the same way. [I'm] not a person that's putting it in your head — 'believe this, believe this, believe this.' I'm going through something, I'm a sinner and I'm trying to figure myself out. It never sounds preachy. It sounds like a person who's really confused by what the world has put upon him.[135]

This mirrors part of the internal struggle he goes through along the journey of the album. The listener is taken through a passage of Kendrick's trials, tribulations, and self-discovery and it sounds like he hopes the listener will have a greater understanding of their own self in the end. By the end of *To Pimp a Butterfly*, Kendrick has transformed into that butterfly, and likely understands the power he possesses from his success and celebrity, and how best to go about making the world a better place.

Early in the album, we find Lucy chasing after Kendrick after providing him fame and fortune. Playing the part of his conscious, Kendrick raps, "what's wrong, nigga?/I thought you was keeping it gangsta/I thought this what you wanted/they say if you scared, go to

---

[135] Andrew Nosnitsky, "Kendrick Lamar Talks Rap, Religion and the Reagan Era," *MTV*, July 11, 2011.

church/but remember, he [the Devil] knows the bible too." In Matthew 4:5-7, the Devil quotes Psalm 91:11-12 to Jesus to tempt him into breaking his fast. Lucy, the Devil, the rap game, whatever you wish to call it, is similarly tempting Kendrick into living a common hip hop lifestyle instead of following the righteous path he is on. Being conscientious that evil lurks around the corner is the first step to avoiding it and staying true to your goals. In "i" he raps, "huh (walk my bare feet) huh (walk my bare feet)/huh (down, down valley deep) huh (down, down valley deep)" which brings to mind the often-quoted Psalm 23:4.[136] Kendrick finds strength and confidence knowing that God is with him on his journey and even if he is depressed or struggling with internal demons, he has faith that everything will be alright.

The music video titled "God Is Gangsta" that came out about ten months after the release of the album serves as a visual accompaniment of a few tracks on the album, and in the video, there are subliminal messages that flash on the screen, the first subliminal message being the number 8. Historically, "8" represents many things including a new beginning, as Kendrick is seen being dumped underwater as if being baptized. Born again, Kendrick is resurrected from the dead into eternal life in the video. Additionally, the New Testament was penned by eight men, Jesus showed himself eight times after his resurrection, and 8 is the number of Jesus whose name in Greek adds up to 888. The Bible says Jesus was selected to take away the sins of all men on Nisan 10[137] (according to the Hebrew calendar), crucified on Nisan 14, and resurrected three days after he was buried on Nisan 17, which is the eighth day after Jesus was selected as the sacrificial lamb. Kendrick, by being reborn into an understanding of his responsibilities, is the sacrificial lamb to take away the sins of his people.

---

[136] "Yea, though I walk through the valley of the shadow of death, I will fear no evil; for You are with me; Your rod and Your staff, they comfort me."
[137] John 12:28-29

Kendrick plays many roles throughout *To Pimp a Butterfly* and although it can be disputed that Kendrick is a Christ-like figure, it would be remiss to ignore the allusions to the Bible and the Christian ideals and influences that are found throughout Kendrick's inner journey.

Kendrick's Complicated Relationship with Lucy

The main antagonist throughout the album is Lucy who, again, takes the role of Lucifer, American history, American government, the music/rap industry, and general temptation. Kendrick struggles to combat this complicated, elusive, and abstract concept as he grapples with this beast of a metaphor. However, the dichotomy of good versus evil rages inside Kendrick to the point where, at least early in the album, he contemplates his relationship with Lucy and God simultaneously, sometimes confusing the two and adding to his inner struggle. In "u" Kendrick says to himself, "You ain't no brother, you ain't no disciple, you ain't no friend" as he feels he has abandoned his sister (who became pregnant at a young age), his community in Compton, and his friend Chad who died in a drive-by shooting. This guilt is expressed by Kendrick angrily rapping, "then he died, God himself will say 'you fuckin' failed/you ain't try'". Instead of visiting Chad in the hospital, Kendrick remembers only FaceTiming him because he was overseas. In Kendrick's emotional state during the track "u", he doesn't believe God will forgive him for his sins.

Kendrick's internal struggle with guilt is combated by his external drive to make his community and the world a better place, especially for the African-American community. In "Alright" the listener is introduced to a version of Lucy who will attempt to distract him from the goal of positive reinforcement within the black community. Since Lucy also represents an America where the criminal justice system has failed African-American people for centuries, Kendrick understands that legality and morality are two very different things in the country he resides as he raps, "I rap, I black on track so rest assured/my rights, my wrongs; I write 'til I'm right with God" indicting that he is going to keep what he is doing as an artist and as a man, despite what outside influences might consider right or wrong. Similar to one of Tupac's songs and claims "Only God Can Judge Me", Kendrick is assured that if he follows his path, God will judge him appropriately. That being said, Kendrick's faith in God leads him to believe that black people will be alright in the end as he says on the track, "but if God got us/then we gon' be alright."

The scene for the track "How Much a Dollar Cost" is chock full of allusions to the Bible. In the song, Kendrick runs into a homeless man at a gas station in South Africa who begs for money. Kendrick denies the man, thinking he is a crack addict but the man turns out to be God in disguise. Kendrick's selfish short-sightedness and lack of charity cost him his place in heaven similar to what is taught in Exodus 14. Kendrick eventually recognizes his mistake, leading to a reassessment about the importance of money over helping others, reminiscent of Luke 16:13 where Jesus says, "no servant can serve two masters. Either he will hate the one and love the other, or he will be devoted to the one and despise the other. You cannot serve both God and mammon (money)." The plot of the song can be compared to a parable in Matthew 25:40 where Jesus decides who he will take to Heaven, and Kendrick quotes the Bible when he says, "know the truth, it'll set you free".[138] Kendrick repents and asks from forgiveness, recognizing his lack of humility as he begins a new path in life. He says, "I wash my hands, I said my grace, what more do you want from me?" which is reminiscent of Pontius Pilate, the Roman governor who sentenced Jesus to death.[139] Kendrick understands that he has been selfish and uncharitable in his life, and wishes to right this wrong and begin a new chapter where he stands up for the less fortunate and the disenfranchised. After being tempted throughout the album by Uncle Sam/Lucy/America/Capitalism/Money/Greed, this song explores the

---

[138] "Then you will know the truth, and the truth will set you free."
[139] Matthew 27:24

true value of money and what it costs, i.e. love, soul, his spot in heaven, and grace with God.

In "Mortal Man" Kendrick asks, "what kind of den did they put you in when the lions start hissing?" alluding to the parable of Daniel. In the parable, Daniel is tested when his friends betray him, and he is thrown in the lion's den. The lion's den represents Kendrick's success, fame, and money; all part of the music industry which tempts him and tells him to act in a certain way. Throughout the album, Kendrick has struggled with the idea that hip hop culture tells him he must be materialistic. The hissing lions may be snakes in disguise, which is a metaphor for Kendrick's paranoia regarding the people that surround him as he continues to succeed in the rap game. Are these people his true friends or simply trying to benefit and ride the coat tails of his success? In an interview with XXL, Kendrick expressed this concern when he said, "artists just get paranoid in any situation and circumstance. I'm always paranoid. I'm already a person who thinks a lot; sometimes I may overthink things or think too much. So, when you're put into a space where you feel like you can't necessarily trust your close ones, that can do some whole other crazy thing to you psychologically. Seriously. All you got is you and God at the end of the day."[140] His faith in God is grounded in the face of uncertainty and Kendrick now understands that as long as he stays true to himself, he won't fall into the traps which have ruined so many in the music industry before him.

Much of the temptation and paranoia Kendrick struggles with is a result of the money he is now making. Uncle Sam and Lucy tempt him on two different tracks with lines like "what you want, you a house, you a car?/40 acres and a mule, a piano, a guitar?" The two characters are one in the same; as the devil tempts with sin, so does American capitalism tempt Kendrick to lose his greater purpose in life. In the outro for "Alright" Kendrick says, "I keep my head up high/I cross my heart and hope to die/lovin' me is complicated/too afraid, a lot

---

[140] "Writer At War: Kendrick Lamar's XXL Cover Story," *XXL*, January 6, 2015.

of changes/I'm alright, and you're a favorite/dark nights in my prayers". The "lovin' me is complicated" line here is repeated from the previous song "u", but in contrast to the frustration he feels in "u", "Alright" shows Kendrick willing to fight and strive for self-love because he has God and the black community by his side. Kendrick then continues the poem that permeates the album reciting, "found myself screamin' in the hotel room/I didn't wanna self-destruct/The evils of Lucy was all around me/So I went runnin' for answers" and indicating that he knows suicide in the hotel room was not the right choice, but still acknowledging that he understands the Devil is after him.

The "God Is Gangsta" music video is the visual culmination of all this temptation, and ultimately Kendrick's baptism and salvation, which take place in the journey of the album. In the video, Kendrick is seen surrounded by beautiful women, tempted by the voice of Lucy which speaks through him as the camera shows him upside down and in a trance while the intro of "For Sale? (Interlude)" begins. Subliminal messages quickly flash on the screen like "Dussy[141] salary cap" and "you'll buy the mall if lust involved, the evils of it all" tempting the viewer with messages about women and money just as the industry/Devil has tempted Kendrick. Everything in the scene is covered in a red hue, indicating this scene is taking place in Hell, as naked women lay him down and rub his body.

Just as "For Free? (Interlude)" is a track about Uncle Sam/America tempting Kendrick with money, "For Sale? (Interlude)" is a track where Lucy is tempting Kendrick with the hip hop lifestyle, fame, and bling. In the first verse, Kendrick raps to Lucy as a lover as he says, "roses are red violets are blue but me and you both pushing up daisies if I (want you)". With the playfulness of the youthful poem, Kendrick is indicating that his relationship with Lucy is based in child-like lust and not wisdom, and the "pushing up daisies" line means that it could lead to his death. The second verse finds Kendrick in his own head, reminding himself of all the ways in which Lucy has and can

---

[141] Slang for vagina.

improve his life in the short-term. Lucy tell him, "all your life I watched you/and now you all grown up to sign this contract if that's possible" as Kendrick changes his voice to indicate that Lucy is angry and becoming impatient because he hasn't agreed to sell his soul yet. By the end of the track (and album), Kendrick has successfully fought off Lucy and recites the poem ending with the line "until I came home" indicating that he will return to Compton.

Throughout *To Pimp a Butterfly* Kendrick is tempted by a variety of complicated elements in his life, all which can be simply represented by the character of Lucy. When the listener reaches the anthem of self-love "i" near the end of the album, Kendrick finally begins to feel confident with what he has learned on his journey and to move forward in life with God by his side. He raps, "the Devil wanna put me in a bow tie/pray that the holy water don't go dry" as an indication that he is surrounded by death, both the potential of his own and that of the many victims of gang violence and police brutality. The image of Kendrick in a bow tie recalls Malcolm X, whose nickname in prison was "Satan". X was assassinated for standing up vocalizing and preaching what he believed in the name of God, and Kendrick fears that something similar could happen to him. However, Kendrick has made it this far and understands how his epic battle with Lucy has changed him for the better. He continues, "dreams of reality's peace/blow steam in the face of the beast/sky could fall down, wind could cry now/look at me motherfucker I smile" as he has faced the beast (Lucy) and instead of blowing steam in its face to delay the inevitable, Kendrick smiles and uses his own positivity and faith to defeat it. His faith in God, the African-American community, and his role as a leader of justice and truth, allow him to smile in the face of temptation and sin as he moves forward into future as a confident leader and spokesperson.

Kendrick as Preacher and Prophet on his own Journey for Peace with Religion

In their cover story on Kendrick Lamar, Complex wrote about how he believes his career is divinely inspired and how God is the reason he was able to escape a rough childhood saying he has "a greater purpose" and that "God put something in my heart to get across and that's what I'm going to focus on, using my voice as an instrument and doing what needs to be done."[142] By the end of *To Pimp a Butterfly* after all the internal battles, time travel, self-assessment, and soul-searching, Kendrick finally understands his purpose and responsibility as an influential and respected artist. The future for Kendrick is to keep continuing his upward trend as the King of hip hop, to gain more listeners, to call out injustices, to teach and preach. In the second verse of "These Walls" he says, "knock these walls down, that's my religion" as he speaks to metaphorical racial and socio-political walls and wishes to use his influence like a religious figure to knock down the walls for the American-American community. Later in the third verse, Kendrick acknowledges how much he has grown and learned when he raps, "take the recipe, the Bible and God". "The Recipe" was a track about women and weed on *good kid, m.A.A.d city* and here he rejects the vanity and temptation of sex and drugs for spirituality. Kendrick has accepted his role as preacher because of the potential wide breath his message can reach, and since he believes his success is divinely inspired, he humbly accepts his role as prophet for his people.

In "u" Kendrick takes on the role of preacher in the way he raps, as if he is preaching to both himself and his audience. Again, he knows he is not perfect and often needs to look in the mirror to hear the message he is sending. At the conclusion of "Momma" he declares, "I can be your advocate/I can preach for you if you tell me what the matter is" to the boy in the song, but also to himself and all African-Americans. He understands that historically, religion has often been used to justify the oppression and enslavement of people but when he raps, in "The

---

[142] Insanul Ahmed, "Turn The Page," *Complex*, August/September, 2014.

Blacker the Berry", "church me with your fake prophesizing that I'ma be just another slave in my head" he is moving forward and understands he can use Christianity to inversely inspire people.

In an interview with The New York Times Kendrick said, "I'm the closest thing to a preacher that they have. I know that from being on tour - kids are living by my music. My word will never be as strong as God's word. All I am is just a vessel, doing his work. From my perspective, I can only give you the good with the bad. It's bigger than a responsibility, it's a calling."[143] Even though Kendrick says he wasn't raised devoutly religious, he has begun to understand the importance of faith and the power of God in his own life and in the African-American community. He often wears a small figure of Christ around his neck instead of a large flashy gold chain that is commonly seen in the hip hop world of bling fashion. In an interview with Billboard, Kendrick prophesized, "we're in the last days, man -- I truly in my heart believe that. It's written. I could go on with Biblical situations and things my grandma told me. But it's about being at peace with myself and making good with the people around me."[144] Even after this statement (it would be interesting to know how he feels about this subject after the 2016 election), Kendrick continues to strive for peace in the face of imminent and consistent resistance from the powers that surround him, because that is what you do in the face of evil and injustice; you fight and never give up.

In The New York Times feature, the article highlights a professor of English at Vassar College who teaches Kendrick's music named Kiese Laymon. Laymon likens him to singers like Marvin Gaye and Curtis Mayfield – "artists who have positioned themselves as prophetic witnesses" and that Kendrick is "reckoning with violence, race, police power and white supremacy […] he's implicating himself in

---

[143] Joe Coscarelli, "Kendrick Lamar on His New Album and the Weight of Clarity," *The New York Times,* March 16, 2015.
[144] Gavin Edwards, "Billboard Cover: Kendrick Lamar on Ferguson, Leaving Iggy Azalea Alone and Why 'We're in the Last Days'," *Billboard.* January 9, 2015.

what he's witnessing."[145] The witnessing and reckoning peak during *To Pimp a Butterfly* as Kendrick does not shy away from the power he possesses when he holds the mic. He is fully aware of his audience, the magnitude of the socio-political issues he is addressing, and the racial obstacles that the world faces now and moving forward into the future. Finally, in "Mortal Man" Kendrick asks his fans, "Is your smile on permanent? Is your vow on lifetime?/would you know where the sermon is if I died in this next line?" He wants to know if his fans are loyal and if they will spread his message or continue to seek it out after he is gone. He knows his role as a preacher, prophet, and spokesperson while he is on this earth, but he wants to ensure that the message he is trying to send continues long after he is gone, into the future.

---

[145] Joe Coscarelli, "Kendrick Lamar on His New Album and the Weight of Clarity," *The New York Times,* March 16, 2015.

7.

Returning Home to Family

The caterpillar is a prisoner to the streets that conceived it. Its only job is to eat or consume everything around it, in order to protect itself from this mad city. While consuming its environment the caterpillar begins to notice ways to survive. One thing it noticed is how much the world shuns him, but praises the butterfly. The butterfly represents the talent, the thoughtfulness, and the beauty within the caterpillar. But having a harsh outlook on life the caterpillar sees the butterfly as weak and figures out a way to pimp it to his own benefits. Already surrounded by this mad city the caterpillar goes to work on the cocoon which institutionalizes him. He can no longer see past his own thoughts. He's trapped. When trapped inside these walls certain ideas take roots, such as going home, and bringing back new concepts to this mad city.[146]

Everything that has been talked about leading up to this chapter was either inspired by Kendrick Lamar's home or leads him back to it. The cyclicality of Afrofuturism isn't only in relation to time or the connection between to the past, present, and future, but furthermore the cyclicality of space is in play, as Afrofuturist artists are inspired by Afrocentric elements of their generational past, but also where they have made their home since the metaphoric alien abduction. The journey from their home planet (Africa), to being enslaved in the American South and beyond inspires Afrofuturist artists to not only time travel, but space travel as well. This allows them to assess where they came from, where they are, and where they are going both individually and as a collective people.

---

[146] "Mortal Man"

Kendrick is currently rooted in California, where he was brought up in Compton surrounded by the history of gangta rap which is associated with the city, but he is also simultaneously influenced by American jazz rooted in the South and the electronic sounds of the future. Globalization and imagination allow Kendrick, as an Afrofuturist artist, to be multiple places at once and just as he can incorporate multiple characters at once utilizing Eshun's multi-ego concept, so too can he pull from the many ideas of home which have inspired his work, namely Compton and Africa.

King Kendrick of Compton

Kendrick understands the importance of Compton to the history of hip hop, he grew up deeply entrenched in hip hop culture and for someone who believes that his success is a heaven-sent gift, to be born in Compton is ideal in the greater sense of what he is trying to accomplish. In "Hood Politics" he states, "came in this game, you stuck your fangs in this game/you wore no chain in this game, your hood your name in this game" indicating that he has taken over as the King of the hip hop game but he doesn't need to wear a flashy chain to prove where he is from, who he is, or who he represents. His hood is his name meaning he is Compton, he is where he comes from, and Compton is the center of gangsta rap. In "King Kunta" Kendrick claims to have put Compton back on the map of the hip hop scene claiming, "stuck a flag in my city, everybody's screamin' "Compton!"/I should probably run for Mayor when I'm done, to be honest". He believes that he represents his home and his people so accurately that he should run for political office, again using his voice for the greater good of his community. This is also represented in the music video for "King Kunta" where he is seen throwing a street party in his hometown as the King of hip hop.

An integral part of Kendrick's connection to home comes from his mother and what she has taught him over the years. In "You Ain't Gotta Lie (Momma Said)" Kendrick's mother speaks to him about staying humble and returning to Compton to preach/teach the youth. The overall theme of the track is that Kendrick doesn't have to put on an act when he is home with Momma or in Compton; he can be his true self. The wisdom his mother bestows, giving him the freedom to be himself, is important in the face of the music industry that tells young rappers they should act a certain way. Kendrick stays grounded and doesn't adhere to the bling culture, refusing to get caught up in the women, drugs, and other destructive evils so prevalent in the music industry, which is personified by Lucy throughout the album.

Just as Kendrick's mother raised him, so did the musical influence within the city of Compton. In August 2011, while performing at a show in Los Angeles, Kendrick was proclaimed the "New King of the West Coast" by Snoop Dogg, Dr. Dre, and The Game.[147] Kendrick understands how big of an honor something like that is, making sure to not take the designation from his mentors lightly. On "For Free? (Interlude)" he makes a reference to the Snoop Doggy Dogg album *Doggystyle* when he says, "every dog has its day, now doggystyle shall help" and in "King Kunta" he alludes to a Snoop lyric when he references "mama and my baby boo too". In these lines, he is paying homage to Snoop as a mentor not only based on his music, but also the longevity of his career. As Kendrick struggles with his own temptations, he can look to figures that have come before them. In "Institutionalized" Snoop raps about Kendrick as if it is the beginning of a fairy tale, indicating both the epic nature of Kendrick's rise to fame and his "throne" at the top of the hip hop world, but also that figures like Snoop can act as a sort of fairy Godmother (Doggfather) to the young rapper. Also, on "Institutionalized" Snoop references the Mozey Wozey, a speakeasy in California that is now closed, as he teaches that what is gone is not forgotten and even though Kendrick has gotten out of Compton, he can never and should never forget where he comes from. He acknowledges Snoop's importance to West coast gangsta rap in the "Hood Politics" line, "I'm the only nigga next to Snoop that can

---

[147] Alex Gale, "20 Legendary Hip-Hop Concert Moments," *Complex*, May 24, 2013.

push the button/had the Coast on standby" using the metaphor of the President being responsible for pushing the button to launch nuclear bombs. Kendrick and Snoop are the Presidents of West coast rap and can blow it all up with the push of a button. Many of the jazz musicians on *To Pimp a Butterfly* got their start playing in Snoop's band as Kamasi Washington said in an interview with Billboard, "myself, Terrace (Martin), Thundercat—we all musically grew up playing with Snoop and the Snoopadelics (his band). I've played on a couple of Snoop's records—a lot of my first gigs. My first major gig actually, I think, was with Snoop."[148] Not only did Snoop have a great influence on the current state of West coast hip hop but jazz as well, and Kendrick collides those two worlds on this album.

Tupac: A Conversation with His Successor

It can be argued, that the entire *To Pimp a Butterfly* album can be heard as one big otherworldly conversation between Kendrick and Tupac Shakur, which isn't revealed until the final track "Mortal Man" where Kendrick inserts his own dialogue into an old interview that Tupac did with Mats Nileskar of Sveriges Radio in Sweden. This is the culmination of the album[149] and Kendrick's internal struggles with fame, his feelings towards the current socio-political landscape of the United States and his own place in the rap industry. Since his idol was killed in 1996, Kendrick never had a chance to ask Tupac the questions he so desperately wishes he could now. However, the interview allows Kendrick to time travel back to a point where he can imagine himself in a room with Tupac, having a conversation and getting answers to questions that were asked to him nearly 20 years earlier, and are still

---

[148] Natalie Weiner, "How Kendrick Lamar Transformed Into 'The John Coltrane of Hip-Hop' on 'To Pimp a Butterfly,'" *Billboard*, March 26, 2015.
[149] *To Pimp a Butterfly* was released one week earlier than previously announced, to coincide with the 20th anniversary of Tupac's album *Me Against the World*

relevant to what is going on in the world today. Police brutality, income inequality, and discrimination against minorities are issues that have permeated American society for decades, centuries even, and Kendrick uses the Afrofuturist aesthetic to show both where we have come from, where we are, and how far we have to still go.

Kendrick's fascination and idolatry of Tupac started at a very young age, as he was growing up at a time when the country was being introduced to the dynamic, charismatic, politically unspoken, rap and movie star. In the years before he was killed, Tupac had become one of the most powerful, successful, and influential African-American superstars the world had ever seen. In an interview for the Grammys Oral History, Kendrick explained how important Tupac was to his childhood when he said, "when Tupac was here and I saw him as a 9-year-old, I think that was the birth of what I'm doing today. From the moment that he passed I knew the things he was saying would eventually be carried on through someone else. But I was too young to know that I would be the one doing it."[150] Outspoken, unafraid, and aggressive in his criticism of America's treatment of black people, Tupac was what the heteronormative establishment feared most, someone that gave a voice to the voiceless, who challenged the status quo, and who was completely unafraid of the retaliation of the people in power.

Kendrick was there when Tupac and Dr. Dre came back to Compton to film the music video of "California Love" and in an interview with The Guardian he remembered the experience saying, "Tupac in Compton, man! To kids, even grown men, he was like a superhero. I don't know what gave him this aura, but he had something else. Now I'm old enough to say I don't think even he knew it."[151] The video, shot in 1995, gave nine-year-old Kendrick Lamar the image of a black superhero, something extremely rare for the 90s and one of the

---

[150] Andreas Hale, "The Oral History of Kendrick Lamar's To Pimp a Butterfly," *The Grammys*. February 15, 2016.
[151] Dorian Lynskey, "Kendrick Lamar: 'I am Trayvon Martin. I'm all of these kids'," *The Guardian*. June 21, 2015.

jumping off points for Afrofuturism. As previously noted, the term "Afrofuturism" was being introduced on list serves at about the same time that Tupac was becoming a real-life superhero for the African-American community. The science/speculative fiction and comic book worlds were dominated by imaginary white superheroes, but black authors and illustrators were beginning to write themselves into the canon and change the landscape of, not only the genre, but of how powerful black men and women could navigate a society built upon discriminating against them. Tupac gave kids like Kendrick an actual example of a superhero figure that was becoming commonplace in Afrofuturist art, undoubtedly giving many black individuals the confidence needed to be successful, challenge authority, and make their communities a better place.

Years later, when Kendrick was 21 years-old, Tupac appeared to him in a dream-like vision, further inspiring him on the path he is currently on. Kendrick remembers the vision this way:

> I was coming from a late studio session, sleeping on Mom's couch. I'm 26 now—it wasn't that long ago. I remember being tired, tripping from the studio, lying down, and falling into a deep sleep and seeing a vision of Pac talking to me. Weirdest shit ever. I'm not huge on superstition and all that shit. That's what made it so crazy. It can make you go nuts. Hearing somebody that you looked up to for years saying, 'Don't let the music die.' Hearing it clear as day. Clear as day. Like he's right there. Just a silhouette.[152]

Although early in his career, Kendrick was inspired by West Coast hip hop artists musically and stylistically, this otherworldly vision of Tupac showing himself to Kendrick from beyond the grave, catapulted Kendrick into a career of social consciousness and political awareness that reaches a height on *To Pimp a Butterfly*.

---

[152] Steve Marsh, "Kendrick Lamar: Rapper of the Year," *GQ*. November 12, 2013.

The cover of *To Pimp a Butterfly* represents Kendrick's rise to the top as rap superstar and real-life superhero just like Tupac. On the album art, where Kendrick and his Compton people are in front of the White House, bringing the hood to Washington, Kendrick says, "[The cover represents] taking the same things that people call bad and bringing them with me to the next level, whether it's around the world or to the Grammys or the White House. You can't change where I come from or who I care about."[153] The reinvention of what society calls negative is part of Afrofuturism. Outkast did it when they put out their album *ATLiens* where they took on alien identities and made it cool and powerful to be different or "alien", Tupac showed that you can be a "thug" and a "gangster" but still have a positive impact on your community and a strong political voice, and on *To Pimp a Butterfly*, Kendrick continues to be himself, including all of his different multi-egos, while still bringing who he is and where he comes from to the forefront of the socio-political conversation in America.

Kendrick also continues to learn from Tupac's life and career, even referencing Tupac's song "Lie To Kick It" in his own song "You Ain't Gotta Lie (Momma Said)" with the line "you ain't gotta lie to kick it". However, Kendrick not only is inspired by the positive elements of Tupac's career, but also the negative, more destructive parts that led to Tupac's early demise. In "King Kunta" Kendrick raps, "ah yeah, fuck the judge, I made it past 25 and there I was/a little nappy-headed nigga with the world behind him" which not only contests the heartbreaking motif that a poor black male will either be dead or in jail by the age of 25, but also alludes to the fact that Tupac was murdered when he was 25. Kendrick is not a thug or a gangster. He lives a humble quiet life and doesn't need to try to be something he is not. Although inspired by the music of those that came before him, he recognizes that if he lives a life leading to his own destruction, he will not be able to get his message across, and his hard work is in danger of being lost to the annuls of history.

---

[153] Joe Coscarelli, "Kendrick Lamar on His New Album and the Weight of Clarity," *The New York Times,* March 16, 2015.

It is unclear who killed Tupac Shakur and for what reason, but with the subsequent killing of East Coast rival the Notorious B.I.G., it is safe to say that the coastal beef and gang violence between East and West was one factor. In the video for "King Kunta", an anthem of pride for his hometown of Compton, the scene opens with a "Welcome to Compton" sign, but Kendrick is seen driving and wearing an LA Dodgers hat but also a New England Patriots coat, contrasting symbols of East and West and an allusion to the patriotism and unity needed in modern America within the black community. As the King of hip hop, Kendrick is proclaiming that East and West need to be united in their fight against things like police brutality and all forms of the oppression of minorities, instead of at odds like in the 90s, which ultimately led to Biggie and Tupac getting killed. The video shows Kendrick sitting on his golden throne, surrounded by his people participating in call and response as they chant "King Kunta".

Returning Home to Momma and Mother Africa

Although the album might take place in the otherworldly realm where Kendrick has his conversation with Tupac, it is still grounded in the reality of Kendrick's real-life struggles, career successes, and his consciousness within, where he finds himself rooted to his home, family, and community. The track "Momma" connects Kendrick's two homes; Compton, where he was born and raised, and his newly discovered home, the "motherland" Africa, where he travelled to in 2014 and found the inspiration for the album. On the track, now that his two ideas of home have been realized and understood, he raps, "this feelin' is unmatched/this feelin' is brought to you by adrenaline and good rap" as Kendrick soaks up how good it feels to be home as he has successfully held off the temptations of Lucy and is back on top of the rap game due to his dedication and perseverance. He continues, "thank God for rap, I would say it got me a plaque/but what's better than that?/the fact it brought me back home" meaning the sales and accolades he receives don't matter as much as how much he has learned from his career and where it has taken him, bringing him back home to Africa and then to Compton to relay what he has learned back to his community.

The hook of the song, "we been waitin' for you/waitin' for you" can be interpreted as the people of Compton waiting for Kendrick to return from Africa and acknowledge his roots in his community, but also for Kendrick to come back to Earth and focus on the real sociopolitical issues addressed in *To Pimp a Butterfly*. The third verse of "Momma" hints that the people of the African-American community are waiting for a person like Kendrick to be an advocate for them at home, while the fourth verse indicates that Kendrick himself has been waiting to acknowledge a greater purpose in his work, art, and life after struggling with depression. Also, in the third verse, Kendrick draws similarities to a poor boy he met while in Africa, connecting himself to his homeland and every African-American who has roots in Africa. He describes the boy as having a "nappy afro", "beady beads", and kicking around a football/futbol. Not only do his physical descriptions of the boy stereotypically mirror his own hairdo in his performance on the Colbert Report in 2014, but by depicting the boy as kicking around a football/futbol, Kendrick is slyly making the connection between the African boy who would likely be kicking around a soccer ball and an African-American who more likely would be playing with an American football. In that description, Kendrick shortens the distance between his two homes, and more predominantly brings his ancestry into his everyday life.

The boy in the song bridges the connection through their shared ancestry as Kendrick relates, "he looked at me and said, 'Kendrick you do know my language/you just forgot because of what public schools had painted'". Western public school didn't teach Kendrick anything about where his people came from, but the language of his ancestors is inside him, and his success in his career allowed him to travel home to Africa and get in touch with that side of himself. The boy instructs Kendrick to soak it all in and learn as much as he can while he is in South Africa as he tells Kendrick, "but never mind you're here right now don't you mistake it/it's just a new trip, take a glimpse at your family's ancestor/make a new list, of everything you thought was progress/and that was bullshit, I mean your life is full of turmoil". This wise boy, possibly a metaphor for Kendrick's childhood self, wants Kendrick to go back to the United States and Compton to make a difference and to tell his friends and fans about what he learned by visiting the motherland as the boy says, "but if you pick destiny over rest in peace then be an advocate/tell your homies especially to come back home". That is exactly what Kendrick did with the album *To Pimp a Butterfly*, and it is mirrored in the final poem which permeates the album and highlights Kendrick's journey home as he says, "so I went running for answers/until I came home" and "made me wanna go back to the city and tell the homies what I learned".

Of the trip, Kendrick told the Grammys Oral History project that, "I felt like I belonged in Africa. I saw all the things that I wasn't taught. Probably one of the hardest things to do is put [together] a concept on how beautiful a place can be and tell a person this while they're still in the ghettos of Compton. I wanted to put that experience in the music."[154] Also, at his performance at the 2016 Grammys, Kendrick finished in front of a picture of Africa that says "Compton" in the middle of it. The bridging of space and time, not only between the distances of his two homes, but of the past, present, and future of the journey of African-Americans, the first alien abductees, taken from their homeland, put on spaceships, and taken to another planet to by enslaved, bred, experimented on, but ultimately to *survive* and become a part of a society that systematically oppresses them to this day, is the story that *To Pimp a Butterfly* tells. African-Americans are going to be a part of the United States of America's future, no longer aliens to be alienated, but survivors and an integral part of the fabric of American culture, art, and every aspect of society.

---

[154] Andreas Hale, "The Oral History of Kendrick Lamar's To Pimp a Butterfly," *The Grammys*. February 15, 2016.

8.

Epilogue

When I started working on this project in early 2016, the United States was in a very different place then when I finished. The 2016 election changed the socio-political landscape of the country, as we elected a President who was endorsed by the KKK, championed by the ridiculously wealthy, and supported by many people who hold white nationalist ideals, making the already tense issues of racial divide even more strained. It is yet to be revealed at what impact this election will have on the lives of many Americans, their families, and their communities, but one thing is for certain, the next four years are going to be quite different from the previous eight, when the first black President of the United States held the most powerful office in the world.

Kendrick also put out another album. *untitled unmastered* is a compilation of b-sides and demos from the time that Kendrick was writing on and recording *To Pimp a Butterfly*. From the cutting room floor of the *To Pimp a Butterfly* sessions of, the collection has similar politically driven and psychological messages and themes, but ultimately would have been out of place as part of the journey of the presiding release. This helps to show how involved of an intentional process the conception and final product of *To Pimp a Butterfly* is when, as standalone singles some of the tracks on *untitled. unmastered* would have been undeniable successes, but they didn't fit the cohesive story of Kendrick's battle with depression and the devil in the face of American racial tragedy and pressure. *To Pimp a Butterfly* is in fact mastered, not only in the studio engineering sense of record production, but also mastered in its thoughtful political and emotional message and its eventual release and reception.

Rick Rubin expressed that he sometimes gets lost in *To Pimp a Butterfly*, despite the plot's linear timeline. Kendrick has achieved fame, is tempted by corruptible forces, faces depression, and psychologically battles back to find self-love and eventually a feeling of home. All the while addressing and unveiling sensitive and relevant issues of racism in America that are at the forefront of the nation's consciousness. However, it will all go back to where it started, when this poignant concept album is considered Kendrick's masterpiece. Where does he go from here? What new pressures resulting from pain and self-doubt will arise? What does the new administration's promises and capabilities mean for Kendrick, the African-American community, and all minorities mean for the future? What will happen next in terms of racial oppression, police brutality, mass incarceration of black bodies, income inequality, and education quality in urban areas? Although Kendrick uses the Afrofuturist move to revisit and connect to the past to examine the present and imagine what the future holds on *To Pimp a Butterfly*, how he views the meaning of those three-dimensional time indicators has likely changed since election day, hasn't it for us all?

> I remember you was conflicted
> Misusing your influence
> Sometimes I did the same
> Abusing my power, full of resentment
> Resentment that turned into a deep depression
> Found myself screaming in the hotel room
> I didn't wanna self destruct
> The evils of Lucy was all around me
> So I went running for answers
> Until I came home
> But that didn't stop survivor's guilt
> Going back and forth trying to convince myself the stripes I earned
> Or maybe how A-1 my foundation was
> But while my loved ones was fighting the continuous war back in the city, I was entering a new one
> A war that was based on apartheid and discrimination
> Made me wanna go back to the city and tell the homies what I learned
> The word was respect
> Just because you wore a different gang color than mine's

Doesn't mean I can't respect you as a black man
Forgetting all the pain and hurt we caused each other
in   these streets
If I respect you, we unify and stop the enemy from
            killing us
But I don't know, I'm no mortal man, maybe I'm just
            another nigga.

-Kendrick Lamar, "Mortal Man"

Bibliography

"Afrika Bambaataa on Afrofuturism," BFI.org, accessed December 4, 2014. http://www.bfi.org.uk/films-tv-people/54afeb7788d05

Ahmed, Insanul. "Turn The Page." *Complex*. August/September, 2014. http://www.complex.com/covers/kendrick-lamar-interview-turn-the-page-2014-cover-story/

"Billboard.com's 25 Best Albums of 2015: Critics' Picks." *Billboard*. December 15, 2015. http://www.billboard.com/photos/6792633/best-albums-of-2015/1

Breihan, Tom. "Premature Evaluation: Kendrick Lamar To Pimp a Butterfly." *Stereogum*. March 17, 2015. http://www.stereogum.com/1787845/premature-evaluation-kendrick-lamar-to-pimp-a-butterfly/franchises/premature-evaluation/

Coscarelli, Joe. "Kendrick Lamar on His New Album and the Weight of Clarity." *The New York Times*. March, 16, 2015. https://www.nytimes.com/2015/03/22/arts/music/kendrick-lamar-on-his-new-album-and-the-weight-of-clarity.html?_r=0

David, Marlo. "Afrofuturism and Post-Soul Possibility in Black Popular Music." *African American Review* 41.4 (2007): 695-707. *ProQuest*. Web. 15 Mar. 2014.

Dery, Mark. "Black to the Future: Interviews with Samuel R. Delany, Greg Tate, and Tricia Rose." edited by Dery, Mark, 179-222: Duke UP, 1994. Web. 28 January 2014.

Edwards, Gavin. "Billboard Cover: Kendrick Lamar on Ferguson, Leaving Iggy Azalea Alone and Why 'We're in the Last Days'." *Billboard*. January 9, 2015. http://www.billboard.com/articles/news/6436268/kendrick-lamar-billboard-cover-story-on-new-album-iggy-azalea-police-violence-the-rapture

Ellis, Josh. "The Trials of Kendrick Lamar." *Rolling Stone*. June 22, 2015. http://www.rollingstone.com/music/features/the-trials-of-kendrick-lamar-cover-story-20150622

Eshun, Kodwo. *More Brilliant Than The Sun: Adventures In Sonic Fiction*. London, England: Quartet Books, 1998.

Gale, Alex. "20 Legendary Hip-Hop Concert Moments." *Complex*. May 24, 2013. http://www.complex.com/music/2013/05/20-legendary-hip-hop-concert-moments/

Grant, Tim. "Soul food: Scraps became cuisine celebrating African-American spirit." *Pittsburgh Post-Gazette*. February 23, 2006. http://www.post-gazette.com/life/food/2006/02/23/Soul-food-Scraps-became-cuisine-celebrating-African-American-spirit/stories/200602230275

Hale, Andreas. "The Oral History of Kendrick Lamar's To Pimp a Butterfly." *The Grammys*. February 15, 2016. https://www.grammy.com/news/the-oral-history-of-kendrick-lamars-to-pimp-a-butterfly

Heintzelman, Katherine. "Oprah Winfrey, Forest Whitaker Talk *Lee Daniels' The Butler*, Racism, and the N-word." *Parade*. July 21, 2013. http://parade.com/58556/katherineheintzelman/oprah-winfrey-forest-whitaker-talk-lee-daniels-the-butler-racism-and-the-n-word/

Hendicott, James. "Kendrick Lamar's 'Alright' chanted at Million Man March for racial equality." *NME*. October 11,2015. http://www.nme.com/news/music/kendrick-lamar-38-1212235

Hernandez, Victoria. "Kendrick Lamar Receives Key To The City of Compton, California." *Hip Hop DX*. February 13, 2016. http://hiphopdx.com/news/id.37036/title.kendrick-lamar-to-receive-key-to-city-of-compton#

Hope, Clover. "The Overwhelming Blackness of Kendrick Lamar's *To Pimp a Butterfly*." *The Muse*. March 17, 2015. http://themuse.jezebel.com/the-overwhelming-blackness-of-kendrick-lamars-butterfly-1691770606

Jenkins, Craig. "Kendrick Lamar *To Pimp a Butterfly*." *Pitchfork*. March 19, 2015. http://pitchfork.com/reviews/albums/20390-to-pimp-a-butterfly/

Kelley, Seth. "Idris Elba Calls James Bond Casting 'The Wildest Rumor in the World'." *Variety*. July 22, 2016. http://variety.com/2016/film/news/james-bond-idris-elba-casting-rumors-daniel-craig-1201820504/

"Kendrick Lamar: Geraldo's Twisting My Message… I'm About Hope, Not Violence." *TMZ*. July 2, 2015. http://www.tmz.com/2015/07/02/kendrick-lamar-responds-alright-geraldo-rivera-bet-awards-controversy-tmz-live/

Kennedy, Garrick D. "Grammy Awards 2016: Kendrick Lamar made history with an unapologetically black album." *Los Angeles Times*. December 7, 2015. http://www.latimes.com/entertainment/music/posts/la-et-ms-grammys-2016-kendrick-lamar-grammy-history-20151206-story.html

Kennedy, John. "Kendrick Lamar's 'Alright' Should Be The New Black National Anthem." *BET*. March 31, 2015. http://www.bet.com/news/music/2015/03/30/kendrick-lamar-alright-new-black-national-anthem.html

Legaspi, Althea. "Kendrick Lamar to Receive Key to Compton." *Rolling Stone*, January 14, 2016. http://www.rollingstone.com/music/news/kendrick-lamar-to-receive-key-to-compton-20160114

Lewis, John. "The new cool: how Kamasi, Kendrick, and co gave jazz a new groove." *The Guardian*. October 6. 2016. https://www.theguardian.com/music/2016/oct/06/new-cool-kamasi-kendrick-gave-jazz-new-groove

Lynch, Willie. "The Willie Lynch Letter: The Making Of A Slave!" December 25, 1712. https://www.archive.org/stream/WillieLynchLetter1712/the_willie_lynch_letter_the_making_of_a_slave_1712_djvu.txt

Lynskey, Dorian. "Kendrick Lamar: 'I am Trayvon Martin. I'm all of these kids'." *The Guardian*. June 21, 2015. https://www.theguardian.com/music/2015/jun/21/kendrick-lamar-interview-to-pimp-a-butterfly-trayvon-martin

Marsh, Steve. "Kendrick Lamar: Rapper of the Year," *GQ*. November 12, 2013. http://www.gq.com/story/kendrick-lamar-men-of-the-year-rapper

McAfee, Tierney. "Kendrick Lamar Vs. Bruno Mars: POTUS and FLOTUS' Favorite Songs, Movies and Moments of 2015." *People.com*. December 9, 2015. http://people.com/books/barack-obama-and-michelle-obamas-favorite-songs-movies-and-moments-of-2015/

Moser, Laura. "Texas Is Debiting Textbooks That Downplay Jim Crow and Frame Slavery as a Side Issue in the Civil War." *Slate*. July 7, 2015. http://www.slate.com/blogs/schooled/2015/07/07/texas_textbook_revisionism_new_textbooks_in_the_lone_star_state_downplay.html

MP. "Super… With Kendrick Lamar," *Mass Appeal*. May 1, 2015. http://massappeal.com/super-with-kendrick-lamar/

Nosnitsky, Andrew. "Kendrick Lamar Talks Rap, Religion and the Reagan Era." *MTV*. July 11, 2011. http://www.mtv.com/news/2694080/kendrick-lamar-talks-rap-religion-and-the-reagan-era/

Oldenburg, Ann. "Wesley Snipes finishes prison time for tax evasion." *USA Today*. April 5, 2013. http://www.usatoday.com/story/life/people/2013/04/05/wesley-snipes-finishes-jail-time-for-tax-evasion/2057455/

Pareles, Jon. "The Best Albums of 2015." *The New York Times*. December 9, 2015. http://www.nytimes.com/2015/12/13/arts/music/best-albums-of-2015.html?_r=0

Parliament. *Mothership Connection*. Casablanca: 1975. Vinyl.

Quinn, Eithne. Nuthin' but a "G" Thang. New York: Columbia University Press. 2005.

Robinson, Collin. "Kendrick Lamar And Mainstream Rap's Growing Conscience." *Stereogum*. January 5, 2016. http://www.stereogum.com/1850795/kendrick-lamar-and-mainstream-raps-growing-conscience/franchises/sounding-board/

Rose, Charlie. "Kamasi Washington." *Charlie Rose*. March 18, 2016. https://charlierose.com/videos/26841

Sarig, Roni. Third Coast: OutKast, Timbaland & How Hip-Hop Became a Southern Thing. Cambridge, MA: Da Capo Press, 2007.

Space Is the Place. Directed by John Coney. 1974. USA: Harte Recordings, 2015. DVD.

Stutz, Colin. "Kendrick Lamar Responds to Geraldo Rivera: 'Hip-Hop Is Not the Problem, Our Reality Is'." *Billboard*. July 2, 2015. http://www.billboard.com/articles/columns/the-juice/6620035/kendrick-lamar-responds-geraldo-rivera-alright-bet-awards

Tate, Greg. "Kendrick Lamar: To Pimp a Butterfly." *Rolling Stone*. March 19, 2015. http://www.rollingstone.com/music/albumreviews/kendrick-lamar-to-pimp-a-butterfly-20150319

Thompson, Krissah and Scott Wilson. "Obama on Trayvon Martin: 'If I had a son, he'd look like Trayvon'." *The Washington Post*. March 23, 2012. https://www.washingtonpost.com/politics/obama-if-i-had-a-son-hed-look-like-trayvon/2012/03/23/gIQApKPpVS_story.html?utm_term=.7278044cd7e0

Vincent, Rickey. Funk: The Music, The People, and The Rhythm of The One. New York: St. Martin's Press, 1996.

Weiner, Natalie. "How Kendrick Lamar Transformed Into 'The John Coltrane of Hip-Hop' on 'To Pimp a Butterfly." *Billboard*. March 26, 2015. http://www.billboard.com/articles/columns/the-juice/6509665/kendrick-lamar-to-pimp-a-butterfly-jazz-robert-glasper

Weiss, Dan. "Review: Kendrick Lamar Returns With the Great American Hip-Hop Album, 'To Pimp a Butterfly'." *SPIN*. March 20, 2015. http://www.spin.com/2015/03/kendrick-lamar-to-pimp-a-butterfly/

"Watch What Happens When Kendrick Lamar Meets Rick Rubin for an Epic Interview." *GQ*. October 20, 2016. http://www.gq.com/story/kendrick-lamar-rick-rubin-gq-style-cover-interview-video

Weiss, Jeff. "Meet Thundercat, the Jazz-Fusion Genius Behind Kendrick Lamar's 'Butterfly'." *Rolling Stone*. April 2, 2015. http://www.rollingstone.com/music/features/meet-thundercat-the-mad-genius-behind-kendrick-lamar-pimp-a-butterfly-20150402

Weiss, Jeff. "Snoop Dogg, Dr. Dre and Game pass torch to Kendrick Lamar." *Los Angeles Times*. August 24, 2011. http://latimesblogs.latimes.com/music_blog/2011/08/snoop-dogg-game-pass-the-torch-to-kendrick-lamar.html

Womack, Ytasha L. Afrofuturism: The World of Black Sci-Fi and Fantasy Culture. Chicago: Lawrence Hill Books, 2013.

"Writer At War: Kendrick Lamar's XXL Cover Story." *XXL*. January 6, 2015. http://www.xxlmag.com/news/2015/01/writer-war-kendrick-lamar-own-words/

Yancy, George and Noah Chomsky. "Noam Chomsky on the Roots of American Racism." *The New York Times*. March 18, 2015. https://opinionator.blogs.nytimes.com/2015/03/18/noam-chomsky-on-the-roots-of-american-racism/

Young, Alex. "Kendrick Lamar delivers an SNL performance for the ages-watch." *Consequence of Sound*. November 15, 2015. http://consequenceofsound.net/2014/11/kendrick-lamar-delivers-an-snl-performance-for-the-ages-watch/

Printed in Great Britain
by Amazon